THE JOY OF
MONEY

A User-Friendly Guide to the Financial Maze

Michelle Doughty
With a foreword by Shirley Conran

KOGAN
PAGE

Nowadays the City is populated with both men and women; the author (ess!) mainly refers to folks in the financial world as 'he'. This is to keep things as clear and easy to understand as possible, and no discrimination, prejudice or bias is intended!

Publisher's note

First published in Great Britain in 2000 by Simon & Schuster UK Ltd

Second edition published in Great Britain in 2006 by Kogan Page Limited

120 Pentonville Road
London N1 9JN
United Kingdom
www.kogan-page.co.uk

© Michelle Doughty, 2006

British Library Cataloguing in Publication Data

A CIP record for this book is available from the British Library.

ISBN 0 7494 4505 X

Typeset by Digital Publishing Solutions
Printed and bound in the United States by Thomson-Shore, Inc

To my beloved parents, Doug and Eva

Foreword

None of us know enough about money. Many of us are confused about *some* financial matters. My recent blind spot was 'hedging', so I looked it up in *The Joy of Money,* where it is covered in one, easy-to-read paragraph; if I wanted to know more detail, it referred me to the Derivatives – Options entry. Again, a model of condensation matched only by its clarity.

This is why I keep Michelle Doughty's A–Z money guide in my handiest bookshelf, next to *Collins Dictionary* and *Thesaurus.* In straightforward, jargon-free language, Michelle explains hundreds of terms from the basics of mortgages and pensions to how to handle HM Revenue & Customs.

I am lucky enough to be a friend of Michelle, and from time to time she has given me instant, sensible guidance on my financial affairs. Having been a stockbroker and run a financial education organization, Michelle has plenty of hands-on experience. I hope that you, too, can profit from her easy-to-follow, wise and simple money guide.

Shirley Conran

Preface

Having worked for a long time in the City and written an investment column for the *Financial Mail on Sunday*, the overwhelming feedback I got from readers and my non-City friends was that I should write an easy-to-read book clearly explaining finance and its terminology, which wouldn't put them to sleep.

There are already a lot of highly respected, competent technical books available about share markets, economics, accounting, etc. My purpose in writing this book is not to compete with them. I just want to make finance fun!

Use this guide when you come across some financial phrase or word that you don't understand in the papers or on telly, look it up in the book and, hopefully, gain instant enlightenment!

Entries are in alphabetical order, and I have aimed to explain what the words in the world of money actually mean. However, anything that's related to pensions is to be found under the heading of pensions. The same treatment has been applied to mortgages, health insurance and derivatives.

Time and time again, we read about people's financial horror stories. The pensions mis-selling scandal is just the tip of the iceberg. I hope this guide will give you the confidence to take better charge of your financial affairs.

Acknowledgements

For their absolutely invaluable input and help, a million 'thank yous' go to Justin Modray of Bestinvest, Roger Bade of Morley Fund Management, Andrew Doughty of Hines Associates, Alex Doughty of CMS Cameron McKenna, Marie-Louise Doughty, John Duffield of New Star Asset Management, Mike Garnett of Hichens, Harrison, Gray Jolliffe and my wonderful parents, who developed editing skills they never knew they had!

Last but by no means least, big thanks must go to Nick Webb, Peter Meinertzhagen of Hoare Govett, Halina Jaroszewska of Coaching For Stars and to all my talented and wonderful friends, too numerous to mention, who encouraged and supported me in my efforts to produce a readable finance book.

AAA – Triple A

In the medical world, a triple A is an Abdominal Aortic Aneurysm; seriously bad news. In the financial world, it is seriously good news. It's a credit rating that is applied to top-quality bonds issued by governments and companies. Triple A status signals to investors that the issuer of the bonds is considered solid and safe and will almost certainly repay its financial obligations. The three main rating agencies responsible for grading these bonds are Moody's, Standard & Poor's and IBCA. On the whole, the City professionals set great store by the credit ratings given out by these agencies as only rarely do they get it completely wrong. Bonds are rated from AAA downwards. When an issuer's credit rating is downgraded, it often unsettles investors as the downgrade immediately throws a cloud over the issuer's financial health. This can lead to investors deciding to dump the downgraded bonds. If the issuer also has publicly quoted shares, the underlying shares may well also be adversely affected and go down in price. A credit downgrade results in the issuer having to pay more for its loans in the form of higher interest rates (see Bonds, Credit Rating).

Account

This is the stock market expression for the time period within which shares have to be paid for when purchased, or share certificates delivered to the stockbroker when they are sold (see Settlement).

Accountant

These scintillating specimens of sparkling soul and wit spend their time locked away in offices and actually enjoy compiling and poring over rows upon rows of numbers. One aspect of their professional working lives is to do the book-keeping for individuals and businesses. But they do get to do more exciting tasks, such as offering us advice on tax-planning and tax-efficient ways of using our money. It's a thoroughly useful thing to have a good accountant. The way to go about finding one is to ask friends first if they know a reliable, trustworthy (with the emphasis on trustworthy) accountant. If not, then contact the Institute of Chartered Accountants for England & Wales: www.icaewfirms.co.uk.

Accounts

Do you have a bank account? If so, you already know what accounts are. The simplest forms of them are our bank statements. They show our financial incomings (salary, etc) and outgoings (usually a lot more than the incomings from spending too much at the sales). Company accounts are basically just the same, with bigger sums of money involved. Money flows in and out of a business; money it owes and money due to it. Whilst we attempt (often unsuccessfully) to save some money, a company looks to make profits and use those profits to expand the business and make itself more successful, as well as to pay dividends.

Every business has to produce accounts. Essentially, the numbers have to tally, accounting for all the money coming in, all the money spent, money stored in assets such as land, plant and machinery, and money owed to other businesses or people. All companies are obliged to publish their results once a year. The bigger the company, the more stringent the rules as to which numbers they have to publish. And if the company is listed on the main Stock Exchange, boy oh boy, they really have to jump through hoops to keep the regulators happy (see Yellow Book). These companies have to show in writing how they fared over the year in an annual report. The regulators insist these results are published within six months of the company's financial year end.

The annual report has to contain at least the following:

- chairman's statement;
- profit and loss account;
- balance sheet; and
- cash-flow statement.

There is one major snag with accounts. Not just the fact that contemplating them is mind-bogglingly dull! The glossy annual report (that costs a fortune to produce in order to impress the shareholders) only represents a snapshot of the business at one moment in time. As it is issued a few months after the numbers came out, it is already out of date. It is easy to make excuses not to bother with accounts because they look so excruciatingly boring. However, dear reader, you have to jump this hurdle. It is important to get to grips with them and where better to start than picking up an annual report. If you are already a shareholder, you have probably seen one for your National Grid Transco or HBOS shares. Tempting though it might be to glance at the cover and hurl it in the wastepaper basket, don't do it. Resist the temptation and instead, open it. Flick through the pages and accustom yourself to reading short little paragraphs. Look for the chairperson's statement and read it. This is where you can glean some interesting information about the outlook for the company. At the very least you'll get an idea of what it does to make its money.

Good information will, over the long term, help you to choose the right shares. If you can get comfortable with at least skimming through the annual report, it will provide a good foundation to enable you to decide whether or not you like the look of a company sufficiently to make an investment. The report gives you a feel for what the company produces, where its major sales are, and who are its most important customers. Remember to take note that it is the consolidated balance sheet and profit and loss of a company's accounts that are relevant to you and not those of the parent company. Consolidated just means that the figures include all other businesses belonging to the company, adjusted for percentages (see Annual Report and Accounts, Balance Sheet, Minority Interests, Profit and Loss Account).

Acid Test

Accounting-speak. Also called the quick ratio, this is a rough guide that measures the ability of a company to pay off its debts if an emergency struck and it had to pay them all in one go. It's one of those infernal calculations that looks harder than it actually is:

$$\frac{\text{Current Assets minus Stock}}{\text{Current Liabilities}} = \text{Acid Test}$$

By stripping out stocks from the calculation, it gives a more accurate picture of just how much 'real' money is in the kitty to pay off debts. A number greater than one is normally good. But be aware: this could mean that the company is sitting on a pile of cash that is not being put to work effectively. Anything less than one, say half or below, might mean that the company is looking decidedly sickly and poised to go up the creek. However, it depends on the industry the company operates in. A supermarket retailer will have a very low acid test ratio because it has such a high level of stock. Don't confuse the acid test with the similar, but different, current ratio (see Current Ratio, Ratios).

Active Management

It's fun to imagine the bosses of a company exercising vigorously to keep in tip-top shape. In fact, active management describes collective funds managed by a fund manager who actively tries to beat a benchmark index, for example the FTSE 100. No easy task. In fact, surprisingly difficult. One of the main contentions of investors in recent years has been how badly many of these funds have performed against a relevant benchmark. Of course, this is partly explained by the fact that funds have operating costs that an index doesn't have. A lot of investors are so disillusioned that they feel it's just as well to invest in tracker funds that do not involve active fund management, but which merely track the index, on the basis that these are much cheaper to get into and seem to do about the same as the more expensive, actively managed ones. However, there is still a strong case for going with actively managed funds that have a consistently long-term good or, if you're really fortunate, stellar performance record (see

Benchmark, Collective Funds, Investment Trust, Managed Funds, Tracker Funds, Unit Trust).

Actuary

Pity the poor person who has to calculate the statistical probability of people dropping off the perch, and then worse still, calculate as accurately as possible the cost of insuring them. Other goodies that they have to suss out include the probability of illness, car accidents, how likely you are to crash when flying your own aeroplane, etc. Yeuch, what a job! Still that's what actuaries actually do.

'A' Day

Financial industry jargon for 6 April 2006, which is the start of the new tax year and the date when major new pensions legislation comes into force. (See Pension.)

Adviser – Dealing Service, Portfolio Management

If you are lucky enough to have lots of money, but little knowledge in the field of stock market investment, it would be useful to get advice either from a good stockbroker, a portfolio manager, or both, who will offer you advice (for a fee naturally!) as to how you should invest your money. Obviously, you should practise great discretion before you enter into such a level of trust with anyone, especially when it means handing over your hard-earned (or inherited) cash to a complete and utter stranger. You should be checking out the following:

- Are they authorized to give advice?
- How long have they been in the business?
- And what's their track record over one, three and five years, or even longer, say ten years?

Don't fall for smooth sales patter (see Agency Broker, Commission, Financial Adviser, Financial Services Authority, Independent Financial Adviser, Portfolio Management, Stockbroker).

AER – Annual Equivalent Rate

One of many TLAs (three-letter acronyms) the financial services companies love to use! This number, expressed as a percentage, tells you what interest rate you'd get on your savings if it was paid and compounded once a year, excluding bonuses. This is the number most adverts highlight for savings products so it means you can make comparisons more easily on what return you can expect, that is, yield, over time (see Compounding, Yield).

Agency Broker

In the stock market, there are two types of broker. Those who are pure agency brokers, only buying and selling shares on behalf of their clients and who do not take shares on their own 'book'. Then there are those brokers who also act as principal, stumping up their own money to buy and sell shares, that is, they act as market-makers as well as agency brokers. If you want to be certain of getting impartial advice or dealing, it is often better to stick to a pure agency broker (see Association of Private Client Investment Managers and Stockbrokers, Market-Maker, Single Capacity).

Agreed Bid

When the head honchos of a company that is being gobbled up by another one, agree to the transaction with the head honchos of the gobbler.

Agreed Merger

When two companies decide to jump into bed together amicably and form one company out of two.

Allotment

Not the patch where you grow your organic vegetables. Allotment is the amount allocated to you when you subscribe for shares in a company that is newly brought to the market. If it's a good new issue you will invariably get far fewer shares than you wanted and feel aggrieved. If it turns out to be a mega-flop, you will get the full amount you subscribed for. Wonder why that is?

Allotment Letter

The official letter that tells you how many shares you have been allocated from a company's new share issue (see Allotment).

Alpha

Beta, gamma, delta. You're probably thinking this is all Greek to you. Don't get fazed. Alpha is just another way of describing a very large, top-quality, or 'blue chip' company, whose shares are regularly traded on the stock market in 'size' (that is, big size).

Alternative Investment Market – AIM

The alternative stock market for dynamic, young, thrusting companies that want to get into the big league, that is, the main stock market, but do not as yet have the track record to make the leap to the big time. The rules and regulations for getting listed onto the main Stock Exchange are very rigorous and strict, so the AIM suits these smaller, young companies. It is important that budding entrepreneurs should have stock market access to raise money for their often fast-growing and cash-guzzling companies. However, from your point of view, as a potential investor, you should be aware that there is quite a lot more risk attached to buying shares in these companies, compared with solid, safe, seemingly boring blue chips. It can be a rollercoaster ride. If things go well, AIM shares will shoot up dramatically. If things aren't going so well, analysts and investors tend to be ruthless and dump them wholesale. Information flow is also not as good as that for companies with shares listed on the main stock market, so the private investor is often the last to know what's going on. Since the liquidity (the ease with which you can buy or sell) in many AIM shares is often not great in the first place, when things go wrong there is often a double whammy effect. A whole bunch of people try to dump difficult-to-sell shares all at once, and you find yourself saddled with them (see Illiquid, Liquid, Nominated Adviser – Nomad).

American Depositary Receipts – ADR

Americans who want to buy shares in non-American companies buy them in a package called an American Depositary Receipt or ADR. Each ADR is traded in the United States as though it is an American share and pays dividends in dollars, regardless of the country of origin of the shares (see Depositary Receipts).

Amortization

In accounting-speak, this is another word for depreciation. However, there is a difference in the way the words are used. You can amortize both tangible and intangible things, like a loan or a lease, whereas you can only depreciate tangible assets (see Depreciation, Intangible Assets, Tangible Assets).

Analyst

City analysts research companies, usually those that are listed on the Stock Exchange. Rather like the local GP who gives you a regular check up with numerous tests and much prodding to find out the exact state of your health, an analyst gets to know the management of a company, making company visits and doing lots of financial calculations to ascertain the health or otherwise of the business. Writing heavy tomes that offer a detailed analysis of companies, they spend a lot of their time being nice to institutions (the big boys of investing), paving the way for their stockbroking sales teams to move in and do the deals. They also spend a lot of time grovelling to these institutions when their diagnoses for companies turn out to be wrong! (see Fundamentals/Fundamental Analysis, Institutional Investors, Technical Analysis). Alternatively, this is the person to whom you turn when the value of your share portfolio halves and you become a gibbering wreck.

Angel

In the business context, angels are the people who put money into young businesses that are still at the fledgling stage. These are usually private investors who back an idea that they think will be a goer. Of course, it goes without saying that there is a high-risk tag attached to this kind of investment (see Risk, Risk/Reward Ratio).

In a showbiz context, angels are the heroes of the theatrical and musical world (or completely foolhardy, depending on your viewpoint), who finance creative people and new productions. If you backed Cameron Mackintosh in the early days, you're laughing. But for every *wunderkind* like Cameron, there are many more duds and non-starters, so beware. It's high-risk, high-reward stuff. However, if you really love great British theatre and want some involvement in it, you can contact the Society of London Theatre, www.officiallondontheatre.co.uk. These guys will send you information warning you of the risks involved, and if you're still gung-ho about it, will put you on their mailing list as a potential theatrical investor.

Annual General Meeting – AGM

As a general rule, all companies are obliged to hold one of these once a year, soon after announcing their end of year results. For the larger, Stock Exchange listed ones it's usually a big shindig where the chairperson, chief executive and directors of a company make themselves available to their shareholders and are obliged to give them a nice little summary of just how wonderfully or abysmally they've done over the previous financial year, and the reasons why. If the attendees are really lucky, they might even get a clear idea of the prospects of the company for the current financial year. It's a great opportunity for investors, both great and small (you can attend an AGM even if you only have one share in the company) to ask pointed questions about things they're not happy with or unsure about (see Accounts, Extraordinary General Meeting).

Annual Report and Accounts

This is a glossy, slick document produced by all companies that are quoted on the Stock Exchange and it should come out within six months of the announcement of a company's results. You get a summary of the company's activities, a look-see at what it owns and how much money's in the kitty, how much it owes and is owed, and how much profit or loss was made for the year. So don't get intimidated by the myriad of numbers because they really aren't as scary as they look (see Accounts).

APR – Annual Percentage Rate

This number, expressed as a percentage, tells you how much you are paying for the use of any money you borrow, that is, credit, a loan, etc. It includes both compounding and any charges you have to pay and means you can compare different types of credit from the vast choice of financial services companies all eagerly bending over backwards to persuade you to sign on the dotted line. Generally speaking, the lower the APR number, the better for you because it means you are paying less for the privilege of borrowing the dosh (see Compounding).

Arbitrage/Arbitrageur

If you've ever been to various shops to compare the price of a particular model of TV to see which shop is selling it the cheapest, this gives you some idea of what arbitrageurs do. However, while you are unlikely to buy the TV with a view to selling it at a profit, the arbitrageur does precisely that. Of course, 'arbs' as they are commonly called in the City, don't trade in television sets, but they do look to exploit the anomalies between the prices of shares (or currencies or commodities) that exist in various marketplaces.

'A' Shares

When you see 'A' shares in a company, watch out! It means that there is more than one type of share, each of which will have different rights and attributes. These can be anything the company wants them to be. Some shares might be non-voting, some might be double voting at Annual General Meetings or Extraordinary General Meetings. 'A' shares are relatively rare, and tend to be issued by family-controlled companies, which hold the bulk of the voting shares.

Asset

Assets are things you own that are worth money. Personal assets could be a house, a bar of gold, a picture, a car, cash, a building society account. I think you get the idea. Shares, too, even though they're only bits of paper floating around – well no, actually not floating, but safely put away in your filing cabinet, with a bit of luck. In a business sense, assets are things that belong to a company. They could be physical – that is, tangible assets such as land or property, or intangible, such as intellectual property, patents or brands. The latter are harder to value than physical assets (see Intangible Assets, Tangible Assets).

Asset Allocation

The professional fund managers to whom we've trustingly handed over our hard-earned cash have to decide how best to carve up that lovely loot. The aim is to spread the huge quantities of cash in funds over a wide variety of investments in order to reduce the risk of losing money and maximize returns. Whilst this may seem an easy task – 'Okay, we'll put a million into a nice castle in Scotland, and how about another million into gold ingots?' – it does require rather careful thought. The fancy City phrase is 'asset allocation'. There are two ways in which asset allocation takes place: by type (also known as asset classes) – bonds, cash, property, shares, etc, and by geography – United Kingdom, United States, France, Germany and so on. So let's say a fund manager decides to put 10 per cent of the money at his or her disposal into France. His or her next job is to decide how to spread that cash – how much should go into French shares, bonds or real estate? Active fund managers make all these intricate decisions. The passive variety decide how to carve up the assets by geography, and once they've decided what percentage of the money goes into the United Kingdom, United States etc, they then use the same methods as the tracker funds (see Tracker Funds).

Asset Cover

This is a ratio that works out whether a company owns enough things by way of assets to pay off its debts, if it had to do so. City analysts love to crunch this theoretical number. It's a delightfully simple sum (for a change!):

$$\frac{\text{Assets}}{\text{Debts}} = \text{Asset Cover}$$

Obviously the higher the number, the more secure the company's financial footing (see Dividend Cover, Interest Cover, Ratios).

Asset Management

See Fund Management.

Asset Stripper

The mind really boggles at this one. What does an asset stripper do? Well, the most successful ones are usually (but not always) short, powerfully built and not likely to show off their bodies. Also known as corporate raiders, they make an absolute fortune in this line of business. They are the Jimmy Goldsmiths and Henry Kravises of this world, who have an incredible knack for zeroing in on companies that are vulnerable to takeover. If successful, they buy up the company cheaply, usually with the view to selling off the component parts for more than they paid for the whole. They target weak companies that might have ropy management or products, but which have some underlying sexy assets, like land, property, or patents, that no one else has valued properly. Shareholders in the target company love it because they get to make loads of dosh on their shares and the asset stripper justifies it as creating shareholder value. Obviously he doesn't bother with companies that have excellent management and are doing brilliantly, because that will be reflected in the share price for the company and believe me, asset strippers like bargains (see Poison Pill, White Knight).

Asset Turnover

This is another delightfully simple number to crunch:

$$\frac{\text{Sales}}{\text{Assets}} = \text{Asset Turnover}$$

It gives eager investors a rough guide to how hard the assets of a company are working to produce each unit of revenue, or sales, and so gives them a clue as to how efficiently those assets are being used. The main thing to note here is that companies in different industries have different asset requirements. 'Capital-intensive' industries, such as car manufacturers, which require lots of equipment and machinery for example, will record lower asset turnover ratios than those that require fewer assets. Other terms meaning the same thing are 'sweating the assets', 'asset turn', 'asset utilization' and 'ratio of sales to capital employed'. The higher the number compared with the industry sector average, the better the company should be doing.

Asset Value per Share

See Net Asset Value per Share.

Association of Investment Trust Companies

Also known as the AITC. A useful organization that does its utmost to clarify to you, a potential investor, the virtues of investment trusts or ITs as they are usually called (see Investment Trust). Not to be confused with the Information Technology sector! It gives out helpful freebie and high-quality, low-cost information on the performance of the various ITs. Eager to demystify (hurrah!) how the investment trust world works, the AITC endeavours to explain how one can differ from another. Contact the association at www.aitc.co.uk.

Association of Private Client Investment Managers and Stockbrokers

Otherwise known as APCIMS. This is your first port of call if you don't have a stockbroker, and you don't have any friends who can recommend a good one to you. They'll send you an up-to-date brochure, which outlines details of private client brokers. But watch out – although they'll send you a list of brokers, what they cannot do is provide you with recommendations on which broker to use. That, dear reader, you'll have to work out for yourself, so tread with caution. Check out the track record of the particular firm you're thinking of dealing with and don't be afraid to shop around. Its website is: www.apcims.co.uk.

At Best

'At best' or 'at market' both mean the same thing – it's when a stockbroker buys or sells shares for you at whatever is the prevailing price in the market at the moment of dealing. I do not like the idea of giving too much control to someone else to make decisions like this. I get the broker to check the price of the shares in the market. Once I've made up my mind what share price I will be happy to pay or receive, I instruct him or her to do the deal at a certain price or 'limit' (see At Limit, Stop-Loss Order).

At Limit

It's generally better to instruct a broker to buy or sell shares on your behalf 'at limit'. It essentially means setting a price limit for them. On deciding how much you want to pay for each Bloggins plc share, do not keep this valuable piece of information to yourself, but convey it clearly and firmly to the broker, who will then transact the deal. Share prices fluctuate moment by moment in the electronic marketplace and it can be helpful to have his or her input and guidance as to what's realistic on this front. 'Limiting' a sale or purchase price can also be applied to other financial assets such as bonds, for example. A similar, but different strategy is using 'stop-loss' instructions to insulate yourself from nasty share price shocks (see At Best, Stop-Loss Order).

At the Money

Here we are in the colourful world of options. But there's no need to get dazed and confused. When you purchase an option, you are simply buying the right, but not the obligation, to buy or sell a financial asset, could be a share, a currency, etc, at a fixed price at some point in the future (see Call Option, Derivatives – Options, Put Option). Suppose you buy an option that gives you the right to buy shares in British Telecom at £10.00 nine months from now. They are currently trading at the same price, that is, £10.00. As the underlying shares are trading at the same level as you have fixed the right to buy them at, the option is 'at the money', which means that you haven't gained or lost money with it at that moment in time. This phrase is applicable to call and put options (see In the Money, Out of the Money).

Auditor

Someone whose job it is to check over the numbers produced by businesses. Auditors are supposed to look out for dodgy goings-on or badly put-together accounts. Most registered companies and all stock market quoted ones have to have their accounts audited (see Accounts).

Auditor's Report

This report is tucked away somewhere in the backwaters of a company's accounts. If you own shares in Squidgetmakers plc, pay close attention to this apparently tedious little section. It's actually very important. If the accounts are 'clean', then breathe a sigh of relief. However, if for any reason there is a problem with the way the company has prepared its accounts, or even worse, a potential glitch with the company's activities, it will show up here as a 'Yes the accounts were okay but… ' qualification. If there are any nasty surprises, you'll be on the ball, ready to take appropriate action.

Authorized Share Capital

The activities of all companies are governed by a legal document, specific to each company, called a Memorandum of Association. Amongst tons of other things, this document 'authorizes' the company to issue a certain number of shares. The maximum number of shares that can be issued is otherwise known as its 'authorized share capital'. However, just because the company is authorized to issue, say, a million shares, doesn't mean it has to do so. But if the directors want to increase the number of shares beyond the authorized amount, they have to ask the permission of their shareholders at either an Annual General Meeting or an Extraordinary General Meeting (see Called-Up Share Capital).

Averaging Down

Something that is very tempting to do when you see your newly purchased shares plummet in price. The idea is that if your shares halve in value, and you buy some more at half price, the overall cost of the investment per share will be a lot less than your original purchase price. This is known as averaging down. Of course there is a catch to this otherwise sensible strategy. If your shares have fallen out of bed, it might be a good idea to question very closely why. If there is a question mark over the management or the viability of the business, you may not want to own the shares at all. That will be your decision. Do not just take it as read that the right thing to do is buy more of the same.

Averaging Up

Amazingly enough, this is the opposite of averaging down! It's when shares that you are skilful enough to buy on their way up spiral upwards as the company goes from strength to strength and you keep adding to your shareholding. But you have to be sure that the shares are set for a pretty long-lasting re-rating. It's easy to get swept up in rumour, market sentiment and euphoria. The main thing is to be certain that the shares you're averaging up justify the hype that usually surrounds their meteoric rise.

B

Backwardation

When share markets are moving very rapidly, such as in the 1987 stock market crash (where prices were falling so quickly that it was known as a fast market), sometimes there are inefficiencies in the way shares are priced. One market-maker (a professional trader who buys and sells shares for his firm's 'book') might be selling Bloggins shares at £1.90, and another market-maker might be buying the same shares at £2.00. An astute trader called an arbitrageur (see Arbitrage) can exploit this price anomaly in the shares, called a 'backwardation', because market-makers are obliged to deal in the shares they make a market in. Oh no, you say, in your kind, caring and sharing mode, that means someone might lose a fortune. Relax. The market-maker is only obliged to deal in a certain parcel size of shares, and he will soon adjust his prices to compensate for his previous error. Or, if things are really looking hairy, the market-maker might just choose not to answer the various phones ringing with dealers clamouring to dump their stock on to him!

Balance of Payments

Every year, the money that goes in and out of the 'bank account' of a country creates a surplus or a deficit. Either way, whether a country is in the black or in the red, the amount of money that is flowing in and out of its 'bank account' is called the balance of payments. In precise economic-speak – the balance of payments records the flow of international transactions of a country over a period of time, comparing inflows and outflows.

Balance Sheet

A snapshot of a company's assets and liabilities on the day the company's financial year ends. It shows you the things the business owns versus its debts.

Bank of England

Nearly every country has a central bank that is responsible for printing those pretty little banknotes that we so eagerly enjoy spending. The Bank of England is ours. Dubbed 'The Old Lady of Threadneedle Street' by the City, she (for naturally anyone who controls the country's purse-strings must be a she!) is also in charge of borrowing cash from outsiders in the form of government bonds, otherwise known as gilts. These pay a fixed rate of return over their lifetime. The Bank of England keeps a watchful eye on the performance of all the banks registered in the United Kingdom, as well as licensing banks for business. This includes foreign banks that want to operate in the United Kingdom. It also sets our interest rates, at arm's length from the government. A group of people meets once a month to decide whether interest rates should go up, go down or stay unchanged. Called the Monetary Policy Committee (MPC for short) these bods hold our financial future in their hands. Since they decide the national cost of borrowing, it also settles how much we'll get while our money languishes on deposit. This in turn affects business and consumer confidence, which influences the outlook for the economy. Governments don't like it if we spend and borrow too much (a boom), and they don't like it if we spend and borrow too little (a bust or recession). They use interest rates to try to control our financial habits, which is unfortunately a bit like trying to do brain surgery with a fish knife (see Base Rate, Boom/Bust, Central Bank, Interest Rate).

Bankrupt

Oh dear, oh dear, oh dear. You really don't want this to happen to you. It's when the bills pile up and up and in the end the unlucky person who's accumulated these debts knows that there isn't a dingo's chance in hell that he or she can pay them. Filing for bankruptcy wipes the slate clean, in a manner of speaking, but there are negative corollaries, such as the fact that getting money on credit can be an uphill struggle in future, and when trying to borrow money, the prognosis is not good. Banks are remarkably reluctant to hand over money to people who have defaulted once before. You might find it impossible to get a mortgage in the future, be barred from being a director, or find it hard to get other jobs. Pensions, inheritance and any other assets you own are also at risk.

However, there are other, more sinister sharp dealings that go on, and not necessarily on the side of the borrower. There is a nefarious practice that goes on with some lenders of cash (naming no names for fear of being relentlessly sued!). It's when they cheerfully lend you money because you have a very sexy asset that can act as security against the loan. It could be land, a stately pile of rocks, a valuable picture, etc. So there you are diligently toiling to pay off your debts, and wallop, the institution forecloses rather too sharpish on the loan by which I mean, they say 'Cough up the money you owe us, or else!' The 'or else!' naturally refers to handing over the valuable thing that acted as security for the loan in the first place. So think carefully before you borrow money against your cherished possessions.

Bargain

Quaint old-fashioned City word that means any transaction in a share or bond.

Base Rate

The Bank of England sets the national interest rate, called the base rate. Then all the banks and building societies immediately react (well, usually anyway) and adjust the rates of interest at which they are willing to lend us money, as well as the rates they will give us when we put the money on deposit with them (see Bank of England, Interest Rate, Prime Rate).

Basis Point

The City calls them Bips. This just means 0.01 per cent. So 100 basis points sound enormous but are in fact only 1 per cent. The need for such teensy-weensy calibrations in interest rates has arisen because such vast quantities of money are being chucked around in the form of loans, bonds, currency trades, etc, that every tiny movement in interest rates can mean the loss or gain of a huge sum of money.

Bear

The opposite of a bull, a bear is the doom and gloom merchant who shakes his head and says the stock market is going to fall. He has usually presciently sold all his shares at what he perceives to be the top of the market and watches with a certain amount of *schadenfreude* as the suckers who still own shares panic and sell them at any price as the market falls out of bed (see Bull).

Bearer Securities

Bits of paper that are valuable and equivalent to cash, these are virtually always bonds (see Bonds). Like cash, they belong to who-ever has them in their hands at the time. In this case possession is ten-tenths of the law! Bearer securities do not have to be registered in anyone's name, so they are nice and anonymous. Just like other bonds, they are tradable, but are becoming increasingly rare these days as it is a bit dodgy to carry around paper of such high value (see Registered Securities, Securities).

Bear Market

When everyone in the whole world is gloomy and the stock market is dominated by traders who are all really negative vibe merchants and dumping shares wholesale, followed closely by panicking investors. Bear markets tend to strike out of the blue when every-one is really optimistic and expectations are high, so when something goes wrong, it scares the heebie-jeebies out of them. They are triggered by a sudden and total loss of confidence in things on a massive scale. People get very insecure and fearful, neither spending nor borrowing money, and this has an enormous knock-on effect on the rest of the economy, plunging it into recessionary torpor. The 'bear' is characterized by the fact that the market falls and keeps falling over a long period of time. One day of negativity here or there is not a bear market. Even a sharp, precipitous plunge is usually described as 'just a healthy correction'. Don't you just love these euphemisms! No, a real bear market drags on and on and on, the sense of doom and gloom is all-pervasive and shares are definitely not flavour of the month or year for that matter. In truth, not many of us have actually seen a really hairy bear market. The last one was back in 1974, when the stock market fell to a quarter of its original value (see Bull Market).

Bear Raid

It's not Winnie the Pooh raiding the larder for honey (although some of the traders do bear more than a passing resemblance to him, on account of the copious amounts of alcohol they consume – purely to help their investment decisions you understand). Those bad boys (and girls) of finance, speculating traders, love getting up to all sorts of spivvy activities to try to get the better of the rest of the market. Bear raiding is when these folks dump huge piles of shares in a particular company on to the market in the hope that they will panic others into selling them. These traders are very often (though not always) 'shorting' ie, flogging shares they don't own. The idea behind spooking other shareholders into selling their shares is to further depress the price of the shares the traders are dumping. Why do they do this? Ah, there is method in their madness. Having frightened everyone else out of their shares the bear raiders furtively re-enter the market and start to buy up all the shares in that company at the depressed price. The shares have been sold at a higher price and bought back at a lower price, so the traders are quids in. Of course, it goes without saying that this is a risky business and these dirty tactics could easily backfire – the traders could sell shares they don't own and the price of the shares could, horror of horrors, start going up (see Bear Squeeze).

Bear Squeeze

This is a bear raid gone wrong. When traders 'short' shares, ie, sell shares they don't actually own, in the hope of buying them lower down, the trade can go against them. The shares they hoped to buy back lower down suddenly swoop up in price, wrong-footing them and leaving them nursing rather severe losses. The reason being that traders have only a limited time in which to buy back the shares they've sold 'short' before they have to deliver them to the purchaser. The longer they are caught short without the shares, the greater the risk that they will end up really paying through the nose when they finally get to buy them back. Of course their competitors whoop with delight at the thought of the bear raiders getting unstuck!

Bed and Partner

Bed and partnering is a legitimate way of reducing a capital gains tax liability (CGT) on shares. The idea is that shares you own at the end of the tax year are worth so much. By selling them on the last day of the tax year and buying them back the next day, you can use up your CGT allowance for the year to the full, and at the same time limit the future amount of gain on which you are liable for the dreaded CGT. The shares are sold in one person's name and when they are bought back the following day, at the start of the new tax year, they are transferred into the name of the spouse. I can imagine a lot of people playing ping-pong with their shares every year in this way (see Tax – Capital Gains Tax).

Benchmark

This word is bandied around a lot in the City. Basically it's a way of comparing one investment with another to see how they have performed relative to one another. The City types like to see whether their recommendations and investments are faring better or worse than their selected benchmarks. A well-known benchmark is the FTSE 100, which measures the stock market performance of the top 100 British companies listed on the Stock

Exchange. Comparing how an investment has performed in this way, you can get an idea of whether it is outperforming or under-performing the benchmark. Obviously the thing to remember is that just as you can't compare apples and tomatoes, so it's pretty meaningless to compare a Japanese share's performance with the UK FTSE 100, for instance (see Outperform, Underperform).

Best Advice

It's the equivalent of the Hippocratic oath for doctors, only it applies to stockbrokers and all financial advisers in the investment community. Mostly they adhere to the rules, but you have to be on your guard against excessively optimistic, infuriatingly chirpy advisers who somehow omit to mention the downside in their investment advice. There is a tendency to – how shall we say – emphasize the positive and de-emphasize the negative. That puts the onus on you to ask the difficult questions. Don't let any adviser off the hook by assuming that because they are being positive and cheerful that they must be right all the time (see Adviser, Financial Adviser, Independent Financial Adviser, Stockbroker).

Beta

The volatility of an investment compared with its market. A share that has a beta of one, for example, has the same level of volatility as its stock market. The more volatile or unstable a particular share is, the higher its beta (see Volatility).

Bid

The price at which you can sell a share on the stock market (see Offer, Spread).

Bid/Offer Spread

See Spread.

Big Board

You might be thinking 'Big Bird' in Sesame Street. No. It is the Big Board that shows the main prices of shares traded on the floor of the American Stock Exchange.

Big Picture

When you start to get interested in finance and business, (and it is addictive, I warn you), it is important to pay attention to what is going on in the big wide world out there. So it means keeping an eye on things such as where US interest rates are heading, and international events that might have a bearing or effect on your local stock market. Middle East unrest is a popular one for causing upset. Obviously it's impossible to predict what might happen in the future as far as world markets go. We can, however, look to history to see how large-scale world events have previously affected them. The oil shock in the 1970s is a good example. It resulted in a huge rise in inflation as costs for industry rocketed, and investors lost all confidence in business as they worried about it, justifiably, I might add. You need to have a heightened awareness of what's going on in the big picture in order to help your investment decisions.

BIMBO

See Buy In Management Buy Out.

Black Monday

The City loves to christen really ghastly stock market moments with a special name. It gives the traders something to talk about when they go for their ritual binges down the frilly wine bars, like Corney & Barrow, that have proliferated in the City since the 1980s. Black Monday is a popular one. It describes the day the Dow Jones Industrial Average fell, okay plunged vertiginously to be precise, by the biggest amount it's ever plunged in the whole history of the stock market. I was there on Monday 19 October 1987 (ah, reminisce) with all the other die-hards and witnessed the wholesale panic and fright. The market's fall scared the living daylights out of everybody, many of whom were convinced the end of the world was nigh and sold their shares. Of course, with the benefit of hindsight (see Jobbing Backwards), all those panic-stricken investors now jovially describe it as a healthy correction, a mere blip in the relentless upward march of the longest bull market we have experienced in the last 100 years.

Black Tuesday

Another gory day in the annals of stock market history. This one, few will remember with any vividness. It describes the Great American Stock Market Crash of 29 October 1929. (You may have already observed that October seems to be a popular month for stock market crashes!) Black Tuesday was, without doubt, the worst day for the 1930s as far as the world economy went. It pre-cipitated the Great Depression, which was a horrible global economic slump. One relegated to the history books (we hope!).

Black Wednesday

When Britain pulled out of the Exchange Rate Mechanism on 16 September 1992, the Chancellor of the Exchequer had already spent a cool several billon pounds trying to defend sterling against the likes of Soros and others, who had been dumping the currency in the conviction that it was overvalued within the ERM. Once sterling was on its own, it weakened a bit more. But like the phoenix rising from the ashes, it recovered, and our stock market and economy have gone from strength to strength ever since we quit. So we should really rename it White Wednesday because quitting the ERM was good news for us.

Blue Chip

In the City, it describes shares in companies that are very big, well known and perceived to be safe and solid. They are generally the companies with the largest stock market values and many companies in the FTSE 100 are referred to as blue chips. But whilst people tend to rely on these companies being stable with steadily increasing profits and doing well, there are occasional nasty surprises. Like the shock plummet in the shares of good old Marks & Spencer in the late 1990s, when it revealed a serious setback in the company's profits and overall direction. That's why diversification, ie, spreading your money over a wide range of investments, is so important. This reduces the impact on your overall portfolio of something going seriously awry with one of them (see Diversification, Shares).

Board of Directors

The people who sit at rather grand mahogany dining tables in wide, comfortable chairs. These are the bods who are elected by the shareholders to run a company and make decisions with regard to whom they employ, corporate policy and what the business should do strategically. Posh titles include chairperson, chief executive, chief operating officer, finance director, director (see Management).

Bonds

Just as you and I sometimes need to grit our teeth and borrow money, the government, local authorities and companies need to, too. Only they don't grit their teeth, they borrow money with cheerful abandon. How do they do it? Well, one way is by issuing bonds. These are bits of paper that are IOUs that promise to pay us back at some point in the future. Aren't we the lucky ones? And if the promise of being paid back isn't enough, they even deign to pay interest on the money they've borrowed. The exceptions to this are zero coupon bonds, which do not pay interest (see Zero Coupon Bonds). In City-speak, bonds are also frequently known as fixed interest securities and sometimes, stocks.

The UK government issues gilts (see Gilts). Companies issue corporate bonds (see Corporate Bonds). To make it easy for private investors and institutions to buy and sell bonds, bond units are generally sold with a face value of £100 (see Par Value).

Confusingly, this is not necessarily the price you pay for them on the bond market. When bond prices go up, the return, or yield you get on them, automatically goes down (see Yield). When bond prices fall, the return goes up. It's an incontrovertible rule, like the law of gravity.

The outlook for inflation (which is the big enemy of bonds) affects the price of a bond, as well as interest rates and the quality of the borrower (see AAA, Credit Rating). Most individuals have indirect exposure to bonds through their pension and life insurance funds. These big funds invest in a huge cross-section of bonds.

One of the things that makes bonds different from shares is that they pay predetermined rates of return, which are not linked to the profits or losses of the borrower. The bondholder doesn't benefit from the profitability of the borrower, as a shareholder would from increased dividends. On the flip side, however, he or she is usually insulated from the borrower's losses.

Bonus Issue

This describes freebie shares given to existing shareholders. Sounds great, but don't get too excited. You might get more shares, but before you genuflect in sheer pitiful gratitude to the management at receiving something for nothing, don't kid yourself for one minute that there is such a thing as a free lunch, or a free share for that matter. No, bonus shares are simply the company's way of issuing new shares with money from its reserves. The fancy jargon for this is 'capitalizing its reserves', hence the reason why this is also called a capitalization issue. When a company issues these bonus shares, it is in direct proportion to the number of shares you already own. A 1 for 5 bonus would mean one extra new share in addition to the five old ones. The number of shares in issue is automatically increased by that proportion and the price of the shares may drop to reflect the increase in their number. Theoretically a bonus issue should improve the liquidity or tradability of the company's shares. Only this doesn't necessarily happen because the shares are still owned by the same shareholders, who might not sell their shares at all. A bonus issue is not quite the same as a share split (see Scrip Issue, Share Split).

Book Value

Incalculable. What? The value of this book. On a more serious note: everything that a company owns has a value recorded in its accounts. This is called the book value and is the value attributed to those assets registered in the accounts at the year end. Needless to say, the values recorded do not always tally with what the assets are actually worth on the open market. The numbers should show the value of the assets as adjusted for use and age (see Depreciation, Net Book Value). Sometimes, especially with things like property or land, the assets are worth much more than stated in the books. Other times, for example when an industry collapses, a company's stock is worth much less.

Boom/Bust

A boom is a period of marvellous economic growth and prosperity, when money is abundant. People are inundated with credit and it's usually accompanied by a property and stock market boom. A bust – a very painful economic contraction – historically frequently follows this and there is a collapse in asset prices; property and share prices are again the main ones to do the collapsing, and the economy dives into recession. The banks do a tyre-screeching U-turn. From throwing money at people by the bucket load and seducing them with absurdly good terms for borrowing money, they put the screws on and credit is remarkably hard to come by. Most of us have been through at least one of these economic cycles and it's a bit like being at the most amazing party of your lifetime, which is followed by a really horrible hangover. Let's hope that governments have learnt their lesson and endeavour to manage the economy in a more gradualist, sensible manner.

Bottom Up

No, not bottoms up! This describes the very focused approach of serious, high-minded investors who place the most emphasis on the fortunes of individual companies when making their investment decisions. Obviously they do keep an eye on the economic outlook for a country as well. However, their main consideration is the analysis of individual companies to ascertain whether or not to invest money into them, otherwise known as 'stock picking'. It's kind of like cherry picking in that they only pick juicy-looking companies (see Top Down).

Bourse

A French word that means Stock Exchange. It's been adopted by a lot of the other European Stock Exchanges.

Broker

See Stockbroker.

Budget – Government/Personal

The budget of a country is just like our own household budgets, only it's done on a much grander scale. Just as the UK government makes plans for the future, so do we. We try not to spend beyond our means, setting ourselves budgets along the lines of 'I earn £x thousand, so I shouldn't spend more than £y thousand'. Of course we almost always do spend beyond our means. What do you suppose credit was invented for? Similarly, the government decides what it wants to do for the country, and then it works out how much this is going to cost. It then casts around looking for means to raise the money through taxes and borrowing. And where does the government go when it needs to raise cash? Why, no surprises there. It borrows it from us, of course, in the form of gilts (see Fiscal Policy, Gilts, Monetary Policy).

Bull

A bull is an irrepressible optimist who believes the share market is on its way up. 'To the moon!' in City-speak. Generally a bull is someone who is stuffed to the gills with shares that he would like to unload on to someone else (see Bear).

Bulldog Bond

A foreign company wants to borrow money. It can issue its bonds denominated in sterling to make them easier to flog to UK investors. These are called Bulldog Bonds (see Bonds).

Bull Market

This is when everyone in the world is a mega-fan of shares. People relentlessly keep pouring their hard-earned cash into them and nobody thinks for one minute that the market could ever go down. It is a world of optimism, and everybody feels good and buoyantly confident about life. The corollary to this is that they spend loads of money and borrow it too. It tends to happen when interest rates are low and everyone is flush with cash. Valuations of shares get more and more out of kilter with reality and everyone makes up wonderful justifications to explain why shares are so ridiculously overvalued. Phrases like 'New Paradigm' and 'Benign Goldilocks Economy' are sprayed around in abundance, especially in the financial press. People are usually too busy enjoying all the extra cash to notice the bolt from the blue that usually puts a stop to all the optimism and heralds the dawn of a bear market. Will there be another bear market in the future? Chances are there will be. Why? Because markets go up and they go down. Of course, we can look to history as much as we like, but the bottom line is that none of us know what the future holds. If a bear market takes hold, we have no idea when it might happen, how bad it will be, or how long it will last (see Bear Market).

Buy In Management Buy Out – BIMBO

Who are you calling a bimbo? A Buy In Management Buy Out is when the management of a company buys the company they are working for with the help of new management brought in from outside (see Management Buy Out – MBO).

C

Cable

It's City slang for the exchange rate between the US dollar and the UK pound.

Call

When the City bods are calling you, it's not just for a friendly social chat. It means they want money, specifically your money. There are situations when you are given the right to buy shares or whatever now, but you can pay in the future (see Nil-Paid Rights, Partly-Paid Shares). When you finally have to dip your hand into your wallet, you are 'called' for the money. Quaint isn't it? If you were delirious enough to dabble in futures, and the bet you made was going against you, the broker you dealt with would sternly issue you with a margin call (see Margin Call). In this case he or she would want more money to act as collateral on the bet, just in case you lose your shirt. Don't get confused between the above and a call option. They are not the same (see Call Option, Derivatives).

Called-Up Share Capital

Accounting-speak. This is the money initially invested into a business. It describes the amount of the authorized share capital of a company that has been issued to investors and paid for (see Authorized Share Capital). Let's suppose that the shares in a company have a face value of 10p each. If one million shares are issued or 'called up', that equals £100,000 worth of called-up share capital.

Any surplus paid over and above the face value of the shares forms part of the company's reserves (see Capital and Reserves, Reserves, Share Premium Account).

Call Option

The right, but not the obligation, to buy a share (or any other financial instrument, like a currency) within a defined period of time in the future, at a price that is fixed now (see Derivatives – Options, Put Option).

Capital

Money invested in things like your house, car or shares, etc is called capital. Capital growth describes the increase in value of investments, usually over time. To bean-counters (the dreaded accountants), capital is the money invested in a business (see Income).

Capital Account

Economic-speak. This describes how much money comes into and out of a country for long-term investment purposes (see Current Account).

Capital Adequacy

Companies that are involved in financial services like stock-broking, banking, etc are required to hold a minimum amount of cash in the kitty, which by anyone's standards is very large. The amount is calculated to ensure that the company's capital is adequate for the risks it is taking, and its clients are always protected from those risks.

Capital and Reserves

Accounting-speak (again!). This is essentially called-up share capital and reserves (see Called-Up Share Capital, Reserves). Capital and Reserves then subdivide into things like share capital, share premium, retained profit and other reserves. The only vital thing to note is that all this money belongs to the people who own the business, ie, the shareholders. Fancy names for this money include: equity, shareholders' equity, shareholders' funds. If you can bear to read the annual report and accounts of a business listed on the Stock Exchange, you'll find all these terms feature in the balance sheet page of the document.

Capital Employed

This is an important one, so pay attention! Capital employed is the total amount of long-term money that is being used in a business. This includes its assets, like machines and factories for example, as well as day-to-day cash and stocks, money owed to outsiders and tax owed. All this can add up to a pretty big number. Investors take a very keen interest in capital employed because it tells them how effectively the management is running the business (see Return on Capital Employed).

Capital Gain

In the event that you are fortunate enough to buy something that goes up in value, whether it's shares or a house, the amount by which it goes up beyond the amount of money you paid for it (meaning you have made a theoretical profit on it) is the capital gain (see Tax – Capital Gains Tax).

Capitalization Issue

See Bonus Issue.

Cash

This little word needs no explanation. When people say they are highly liquid, they're not referring to their bender down at the pub! It means that they've got lots of lovely cash at their disposal. Cash is an asset, and the more we have, the better. In company accounts, it is described as a current asset because it's readily usable to pay for things. Shares and bonds are the two other assets that lend themselves to being quickly convertible into cash, that is, as long as they are the best quality ones.

Cash Flow

It's the 'real' money that is actually ringing in the till of a business on a day-to-day basis. It's different from profits because a business can be theoretically profitable, ie, selling its goods for more than they cost. However, its cash flow might be really bad because, for example, the people buying the goods might take a very long time to pay. So even if a company is profitable, it can still go bust if poor cash flow creates a short-term solvency crisis (see Cash-Flow Statement, Price/Cash Flow Ratio).

Cash-Flow Statement

The cash-flow statement for a business is a bit like your bank statement, which records all the money going in and out of your account over a period of time. This statement clearly shows which bits of the business have brought in cash, and where the incoming money has been spent. Without this information, management wouldn't know how much money it has at its disposal to spend on expansion of the business, etc (see Accounts, Cash Flow, Profit and Loss Account).

Central Bank

Most countries have a central bank that controls the amount of money printed and in circulation, and keeps a benevolent eye over the financial system, like a watchdog. The Bank of England (see

Bank of England) has this hallowed task here, whereas Europe now has the European Central Bank doing the same thing for the euro (see Euro).

Everyone takes serious notice of the American Federal Reserve Bank, which is the most powerful central bank in the world. Presently the big cheese running it is Alan Greenspan. When he speaks, the whole world listens. The City watches like a hawk as he and the Federal Open Markets Committee decide US interest rate policy. His decisions can affect the world stock markets, but thankfully, he seems to judge the mood right pretty much all of the time, which is why he's definitely achieved 'guru' status (see Guru). However, managing the world's largest economy is a precariously balanced thing. If he gets it slightly wrong, it can have a devastating effect on global confidence, which would have a negative effect on stock markets, and in turn, economies.

Certificate of Deposit – CD

These are like cash. CDs are receipts given by a bank or a discount house for cash deposited with them. Bits of paper issued in bearer form, they entitle the owner to the interest paid. They are tradable and can also be handed over to someone else. Note that a CD for £10,000 is worth £10,000 and shouldn't be left floating freely around the house. Lock it away into a safety deposit box or the like. Because the sums of money on deposit are quite large, banks use them to get good rates of interest for longer periods of time. Individuals can buy these through a stockbroker, a money broker, a discount house or a bank. CDs are suitable for those with fairly large amounts of money to tuck away (see Bearer Securities).

Chairman's Statement

When you're flicking enthusiastically through the accounts of Bloggins plc, this is one of the bits that will help you to suss out whether or not they are doing well. Bad news is frequently wrapped up in careful wording: 'Results came below our projected expectations' can sometimes stand for the management making a bit of a pig's ear of things. If there isn't a chairman's statement, there'll be a directors' report. If you are really zealous and manage to compare the results of the same company over a few years (yes, I know it's deadly dull) you'll also work out whether the chairman is biased towards being too go go go and positive or too glum and gloomy (see Accounts).

Chartism

See Technical Analysis.

Children's Bonus Bonds

Okay, so it's fair to assume that these are for children, because of the give-away title. But what are they? Well, they're one of the government's National Savings products (See National Savings Certificates), which are equivalent to a building society deposit account with an important plus point. They're tax-free. You hand the money on behalf of your child over to them and in return get a bit of paper that is like a receipt, thereafter receiving a fixed rate of interest on the sum deposited for five years. Visit the website: www.nationalsavings.co.uk.

Chinese Walls

You have probably already guessed that these are not real walls. Unlike the Great Wall of China, these are invisible walls that make sure price-sensitive information about a client remains confidential, and within its own department. They are necessary because the various City activities, such as stockbroking, market-making, fund management and corporate finance, are now frequently housed under the same roof. The same company could be giving a company corporate advice about its business strategy, as well as making a market in its shares.

Example: suppose the corporate finance department is advising a company to bid for Bloggins plc. If the stockbrokers in the same firm got to hear about the bid, the temptation might be to recommend Bloggins shares to their clients, or possibly buy some for themselves. Excuse me, insider dealing? Sharp intake of breath. Indignation and vehement protestation ensues. Such dodgy goings on in the City are unthinkable! City firms assure us that their Chinese Walls are as effective as mega-strong flea powder, stopping information hopping from one person to another, and making sure it stays confidential (see Compliance, Inside Information, Insider Dealing).

Churning

This is the disreputable and thoroughly awful practice of some, but hopefully not too many, stockbrokers who buy and sell shares on behalf of their clients too frequently, with the mercenary aim of generating commission. If you let someone do this with your share portfolio, it will surely end up in a sloppy gooey mess, that's if there's anything left at the end at all. It is why it's very important to keep a track of what is happening to your money, especially if you've entrusted a stockbroker to deal with it on a discretionary basis. This effectively means they have pretty much total control over how they spend your money (see Discretionary – Dealing).

City Code

This came into being because the ever-increasing takeovers of companies on the Stock Exchange led to some rather nasty skulduggery and dirty play by the bosses of the predators that simply wasn't cricket. To stop companies slugging it out and indulging in dirty tactics when trying to buy other companies, the Takeover Panel was created (see Takeover Panel), which introduced an ethical code of conduct to ensure maximum integrity in future takeovers and stock market flotations, etc.

Clawback

HM Revenue & Customs – can you countenance it? – can actually claw back money that it previously allowed for tax relief purposes if something happens to alter your entitlement to tax relief. It's a retrospective imposition of tax. Talk about changing the goal posts!

In the City sense, the word has a more positive meaning, you'll be glad to know. When a company issues new shares, a clawback entitlement means that existing shareholders are given the right to buy the shares first. Even if the new investors have already bought up all the shares, the existing shareholders can 'claw' back their allocation. The corporate broker in charge of the new issue of the shares normally handles this clawback arrangement.

Clearing Banks

They are also known as retail or commercial banks. However, not all retail or commercial banks are clearers. As if you didn't already know, these banks deal with companies, as well as retail customers like you and me. They take deposits and lend money, some at a better rate than others, and offer a whole panoply of other services, including corporate finance, investment and corporate banking, etc.

Closed-End Funds

A fund is just lots of people's money pooled into one fund that is managed by a professional fund manager. The important point to register with the closed-end variety is that it only has a fixed amount of units or shares in it, which never changes. The shares of closed-end funds are traded openly on the stock market, so their value goes up and down according to supply and demand; they can trade at a premium (higher than) or a discount to (lower than) the value of the assets in the fund, otherwise known as its net asset value. Investment trusts are closed-end funds (see Investment Trust, Net Asset Value, Open-End Funds).

Cold Call

Uh oh. If you get a cold call, which is a call from the blue from a total stranger trying to flog you something in the investment field, you should just politely say, sorry you're not interested in the venture, whatever it is, and put the phone down. If someone keeps bugging you, report him or her to the Financial Services

Authority because what they're doing is illegal (see Financial Services Authority).

Collective Funds

Millions of people elect to pool their money into large funds such as unit trusts, investment trusts, tracker funds, etc. These are all different types of collective funds. They spread the cash (hence the risk) over a very wide range of shares and assets, which the individual's small amount of money couldn't possibly do. Why? Because the cost of spreading our relatively paltry sums of money over the wide range of assets that funds hold would be prohibitively expensive. They get massive economies of scale; the larger the fund, the cheaper it gets to buy and sell shares. Whilst we pay commission of, say, 1.5 per cent per share transaction, the funds might pay 0.2 or 0.3 per cent, simply because of the sheer volume of money that they are throwing around (see Active Management, Investment Trust, Managed Funds, Tracker Funds, Unit Trust).

Commission

Something you have to pay if you want to buy and sell shares or get someone to professionally manage your money. Also, when you ask independent financial advisers (IFAs) for advice on a mortgage, health insurance, or life insurance, be absolutely clear that they are not altruists and they can earn very generous commissions for their advice. Endowment policies and investment bonds pay advisers very high commissions in particular. The good news is that new rules mean that IFAs must offer you the option of fees-driven advice or commissions. It's a good idea to check what the advice is going to cost you in pounds and pence in order to satisfy yourself that you are not just paying commission in the form of 'fees' (see Independent Financial Adviser, Stockbroker).

Commodities

Just as there is a Stock Exchange, so there is a commodity exchange, where commodities are traded. The kinds of commodities traded there are raw materials. 'Soft' ones include coffee, cocoa, sugar, soya, even pork bellies. 'Hard' ones include gold, silver, copper, lead, zinc, etc.

Common Stock

See Shares.

Company Share Option Plan

See Employee Share Option Plan – ESOP.

Compliance

'Hullo, 'ullo, 'ullo. What's a nice stockbroker like you doing with this rather tasty bit of inside information? You're not going to do a spot of insider dealing on me, are you, my son?' Hopefully not, or it's go to jail, do not pass go and certainly do not collect £200.

Compliance is the department in a big stockbroking or investment banking firm that has the unfortunately dreary task of nit-picking and checking that everybody within the organization follows the rules and doesn't take advantage of their privileged position to, heaven forbid, make money. But I thought that's why everyone works in the City, guv. There couldn't possibly be any other reason to work in that goldfish bowl, could there? Surely not job satisfaction? Unless I've really got it wrong and the City is populated with the most altruistic souls in the country. Anyway, I digress. The compliance department keeps its beady eye on the activities of its staff and makes sure they don't do illegal things like insider trading, etc (see Chinese Walls, Front Running, Inside Information, Insider Dealing).

Composite Interest Rate

The favourite ploy of building societies is to show off with loud proclamations of 'Come and save with us, get 6 per cent here!' Of course as soon as you are lured into putting your hard-earned cash into their savings accounts, loud cries of indignation ensue when you get your interest statement. Hey, you cry, how come you said I was going to get 6 per cent but I've only got 4 per cent? Well, did you really think the UK government would just let you hang on to all the interest (called the gross interest) without saying a dicky bird? With tremendous consideration and thoughtfulness, just in case you forget to pay it later on, they lop a composite tax rate off the money upfront before it reaches you. This tax is just a bit lower than the basic rate of income tax. Oh, and if you happen to be a higher-rate tax-payer, don't think they'll neglect you there. You'll have to pay back to the government the differential between the composite rate tax and the higher band of tax.

Compounding

Oh, the wonderful effects of compounding. This is when interest earns interest. Say you have £100 on deposit in year one. It is earning 10 per cent interest. In year two, you will have £110 on deposit, earning interest. Each year, interest will be earned on the higher, aggregate figure. Over the long-term, this has a very significant effect on the value of money saved or invested.

Conglomerate

This type of company is also called a diversified industrial. It is one that has gobbled up all kinds of businesses that have a wide spread of activities, usually unrelated to one another. A good example would be a company that owned a bottle-top manufacturing business, a power-drill making company, as well as a fruit importer.

Consideration

Something you may feel your financial experts don't give you enough of. When you buy or sell shares or bonds, you pay for them or receive money. The consideration, rather considerately, is the amount you pay or get before commission charges and stamp duty.

Consolidated Profit and Loss Account

See Profit and Loss Account.

Consols

Before your imagination really takes flight and you start thinking *Starship Enterprise* space age consol, let me console you. That it isn't. This is a City colloquialism for government consolidated bonds. The popular name for a government bond is gilt. Consols are unusual in that they are bonds issued by the government's consolidated fund, not the treasury. As they were issued in the Napoleonic era, they are all undated, ie, there is no date by which the government has to pay the money back to the lender.

Contingent Liabilities

Accounting-speak again. These are debts that may or may not materialize for a company and are terribly nebulous by nature. A company has to mention the possibility of this in its accounts by way of a footnote, though let's face it, it isn't exactly going to advertise the fact that a horrible big hole might appear in its profits, is it? It's up to the investor reading the accounts of a company to try to assess what might be the worst case scenario. A little footnote mentioning guarantees of major liabilities in the future or an impending legal case can be worrying.

Contract

When you buy options in shares or other financial things like currencies, you buy them in contracts. Each contract is always the same size. An options contract in a FTSE 100 share, for example, consists of 1,000 shares (see Derivatives – Options).

Contract Note

When you buy or sell shares from a stockbroker, they have to send you a bit of paper that tells you all the details about the share deal. Boring but necessary stuff, like the time and date they dealt for you, the amount of money you have to pay and when you have to pay them. You'll be liable for stamp duty if you've bought shares. It's a good idea to hang on to this bit of paper for the far-flung future when you might want to sell your shares and have to calculate the amount of grim capital gains tax that you'll have to pay. Which, in a way, is good news because it means that the shares have gone up in value (see Settlement, Tax – Capital Gains Tax).

Contracts For Difference

See Derivatives.

Conversion Premium

This phrase is related to that hybrid investment, the convertible (see Bonds, Convertibles). By now you've sussed that a convertible is just a bond that gives you the right to convert it into shares at some point in the future. The conversion premium describes the amount by which the bond looks overvalued. Why should it become overvalued, you ask? Because when investors like the look of the underlying shares of a company that has convertibles on offer, they pile into them *en masse* in raptures of delight because they are hooked by the attractions of the right to 'convert' the convertible bonds into shares. This drives the price of the convertibles up, thus creating the 'conversion premium'. The investors are thrilled to bits as they're getting the fixed return of a bond, with the added excitement of making money on the underlying shares as and when they convert it into shares. If a convertible isn't displaying a conversion premium, then take it as read that investors aren't in the least bit enthused about converting it into shares (maybe the shares look dreary and dull) and they are viewing the convertible as a pure bond.

Conversion Rights

This just describes the right to convert a bond into shares.

Convertible Loan Stock

Loan stock is just another way of describing corporate, or company bonds (see Corporate Bonds). Convertible loan stock differs from the above in one important way. Instead of automatically paying you, the lender, back the money owed to you at the end of the life of the loan, the borrower can elect to convert the loan into its shares and give you the shares instead. This is hunky dory if all is going well for the company, but rather unpleasant if the shares are bombed out!

Convertible Preference Shares

By now you are savvy with the idea that a preference share is not like an ordinary share at all. It is really more like a bond that pays a fixed dividend to the owner, and in the event of a company going bust, a preference shareholder is in line to be repaid before an ordinary shareholder. And you know what a convertible is (see Convertibles). So it follows that a convertible preference share just lets you convert what is effectively a bond into a share at some point in the future. There are usually certain fixed times and prices at which this can be done, but you can see the attraction for some people who don't like to take excessive risks. The hybrid attraction of these is the same as for convertibles (see Bonds, Preference Shares, Shares).

Convertibles

A convertible is a bond that gives you the option to convert it into shares at certain fixed times. As a bond, it pays a fixed rate of interest to the lender, but with the added spice of the investor being able to convert it into a share at a fixed price at some point in the future if it is favourable for him to do so. It's like hedging your bets. Obviously this type of investment often gives holders the best of both worlds. They get a bond, which can turn into a share. And it goes without saying that they'll only convert the bond into shares if it's in their interest to do so (see Bonds, Conversion Premium, Shares).

If a City trader offers to sell you his convertible, think twice before accepting. It might not be that sexy soft-top Mercedes SL500 you would give your right arm for. It might just be a forlorn piece of paper that looks suspiciously like an IOU.

Corporate Bonds

Bonds are mainly issued by governments and companies looking to borrow money, effectively they are bits of paper that are IOUs. The UK government issues gilts and companies issue corporate bonds. Another phrase for corporate bond is 'loan stock', but you will find that corporate bond is the more commonly used. There are different classes of these, the most secure being a debenture, followed by secured loan stock and the obviously less secure unsecured loan stock. Because there is an element of risk attached to lending money to companies, they compensate for this risk by offering interest rates that are better than the interest paid by building society deposits or government bonds, which are effectively perceived to be risk-free, as nine-and-a-half times out of ten they are. Just as with most other bonds, the company usually fixes a set date to redeem the loan, and in the meantime, they make regular interest payments to the lender (see AAA, Bonds, Credit Rating, Gilts).

Corporate Earnings Growth

This is an important number that City analysts watch obsessively like hawks. Companies listed on the Stock Exchange issue their main results once a year, with quarterly updates for the really big companies. What analysts obsess over is not the actual number, ie, not the £5m Bloggins plc is making this year, but its progress, ie, how much did profits grow by? Is that £5m substantially more than it was last year? Was growth reasonable, given the inflation rate and other economic factors? A paltry 2 per cent qualifies as stagnation, but if profits roared ahead by 20 per cent, analysts are in nirvana. I don't need to tell you how fickle they can be if a company fails to deliver. Merciless with companies that show a glimmer of a fall in profits, they slash profit forecasts, and this in turn means that a company can go from 'darling glamour' to 'nobody loves me anymore' and it is dumped wholesale, leading to its share price collapsing. Then, rather predictably of course, the shares become oversold. And guess what? Those same analysts who gasped with horror at the slight hiccup in corporate earnings growth for Bloggins plc are on the rampage again, advising everyone to pile in because the shares now look cheap! As long as the forecasts for corporate earnings growth keep changing, it's great for the City stockbrokers because the institutions pile in and out of shares as they are told to. The brokers earn their fees on the 'buy' and 'sell' side, so they win either way! (See Earnings per Share, Price/Earnings Ratio.)

Corporate Finance/Financier

This is the department in the investment banking world (see Investment Bank) that is populated with busy worker bees called corporate financiers. These individuals are usually very wan and pale, on account of the fact that they never see the light of day. Corporate finance is without doubt the most gruelling job in the City, much worse than stockbroking. What these poor people do is all the work behind transactions involving companies. They help companies to raise money via the stock market, or advise them on what businesses to buy up or which businesses to sell. Working with accountants and lawyers, corporate financiers make sure that deals go smoothly. And very often, they do tons of work on a project that involves endless due diligence (see Due Diligence, Investment Bank – Mergers & Acquisitions).

Of course there are compensations for this very unsociable existence. Corporate finance departments get paid a truckload of money in fees, but before you get too envious, remember that they only get those dazzling fees if the deal comes off. When a transaction fails to materialize, these guys get a miserable little fee for all their blood, sweat and tears. Don't you want to weep at the injustice of it all? Someone should set up a benevolent fund for burnt-out corporate financiers.

Corporate Governance

This is the posh-sounding phrase of the moment that basically stands for the management of a company ensuring that they act in the shareholders' best interests, and at the same time do the 'right thing', ie, run it with integrity. It deals with very complex issues, like environmental stuff, so bad corporate governance would be doing something like dumping toxic waste into rivers even though it would technically enhance shareholder value, because of course doing that would save the company money, which in turn would mean there would be more money to pay dividends to shareholders. But it's still a no no in good corporate governance terms. And of course Enron goes down in history as a company where corruption and hidden losses equalled very bad corporate governance indeed!

Coupon

Not the Green Shield stamps you may remember collecting all those years ago. Nope. This is a physical coupon all right, in that you get to detach it, as you would a stamp from the perforated paper it is attached to. But the bit of paper in question is a bond. The coupon is one of a series that you have to detach from the bond to get its interest payments (see Bonds).

Covered Warrants

See Derivatives.

Crash

A crash can follow an extended period when all share prices have been going up and up without any really good fundamental reason behind the rise, such as good growth in profitability. The excessive optimism and euphoria driving it has a manic feel (see Financial Manias) and everybody in the whole world seems convinced that the stock market is going to the moon. Then a bolt from the blue will strike that suddenly shatters this ebullient confidence. People get all fearful and insecure, and there is a stampede for the exit. The mass exodus out of shares causes a precipitous fall in share prices, which is called a stock market crash. These crashes, which happen from time to time, are exacerbated by the fact that the professional traders, who deal minute by minute and have nerves of steel, then see an opportunity to make money by heavily 'shorting' stock (see Short). And then the futures girls and boys wade in and do the same (see Derivatives – Futures, Hedge Funds), and the market plunges even more steeply, scaring investors even more. Small investors need to be strong-minded and often, instead of panicking out of good-quality shares, they'd be better off taking a big slug of brandy and doing what the professionals do, which is to take advantage of the weak market to buy the best-quality shares at the lowest possible prices.

Creditors

Gulp. Let's hope you keep these to the bare minimum. Your creditors are the people to whom you owe money. The creditors of a business are the people to whom the business owes money, such as suppliers, banks, H M Revenue & Customs etc.

Credit Rating

It's not just you and me who are checked out for our creditworthiness, but companies and countries are too. This is because they borrow money (in the form of bonds and loans) on such a large scale, that the lenders like to have some idea as to how likely, if at all, the borrower is to default. So three main credit rating agencies (Standard & Poor's, Moody's and Fitch IBCA) check out their creditworthiness. These agencies have teams of number crunchers continually analysing and sweating over company accounts and the like. In doing so they're assessing how risky it is for you and me to lend our hard-earned cash to various borrowers. They have devised scoring points to assess the riskiness of lending. The highest rating is usually triple A (AAA) to indicate minimal credit risk, and the scale goes steadily down as the risk of lending increases (see AAA, Bonds, Corporate Bonds, Gilts).

CREST

Not the pale-blue toothpaste that's guaranteed to prevent your teeth dropping out, but a paperless system of dealing with the settlement of shares. Settlement is the tedious, but necessary admin that's required when you've bought or sold shares. You can hold these on electronic file with CREST if you choose. Alternatively, if, like me, you rather enjoy owning bits of paper called share certificates, CREST obligingly sends those out to shareholders, too. The system is run by CrestCo Ltd, now owned by the Euroclear group, website: www.euroclear.com (see Account, Dematerialized Shareholding, Settlement).

Cum

In a Stock Exchange sense, this just means 'with', as opposed to 'without'.

Cum-Capitalization

When you buy shares that are quoted 'cum-capitalization', it means you are entitled to get the freebie or 'bonus' shares that the company has just issued to its existing shareholders (see Bonus Issue). The financial press symbolize the term as 'cc' and it's found next to the share price details in the newspaper (see Ex-Capitalization).

Cum-Dividend

When you buy shares or bonds and they are 'cum-dividend', this means that you, as the new owner of them, are entitled to receive the next dividend to be paid. The financial press symbolizes the term as 'cd' and it's found next to the share price details in the newspaper (see Ex-Dividend).

Cum-Rights

When you buy shares 'cum-rights' it means you have the right to participate in anything that's going on with the company specifically at that time. It could be a rights issue, a bonus issue or a dividend payout, etc. When you are not entitled to these things it's called 'ex-rights'. In the financial press, cum-rights is signalled as 'cr', and ex-rights is 'xr' (see Ex-Rights).

Cumulative Preference Shares

These are preference shares with a little extra safeguard attached. If the company that issued these experiences a problem in paying its dividends to shareholders, then as soon as it can pay dividends again, cumulative preference shareholders are in line to receive any outstanding dividends before ordinary shareholders do so (see Preference Shares).

Current Account

Economic-speak. This describes how much money comes in and out of a country in terms of short-term trade flows, ie, goods and services, etc (see Capital Account).

Current Assets

Accountancy-speak describing those things owned by a business that most closely resemble cash in its portfolio, or could become cash in a short period of time, usually within one year. It includes cash, of course. They are to be found in the balance sheet of a company's accounts.

Current Liabilities

What a business owes other people, and which are due to be paid within one year. The numbers are to be found in the balance sheet of a company's accounts.

Current Ratio

This is yet another City number to crunch. It's a relation of the acid test ratio. The purpose behind it is to give a very rough and ready guide to see whether a business is solvent, ie, has enough cash to pay its bills. It's a nice easy one to wrap your head around, thank goodness. The mathematical equation is:

$$\frac{\text{Current Assets}}{\text{Current Liabilities}} = \text{Current Ratio}$$

Obviously, a number greater than one is good, whereas less than one starts to look a bit shaky. The acid test is simply a more stringent version of the current ratio (see Acid Test Ratio, Current Assets, Current Liabilities, Ratios).

Cycle – Business/Trade

Economies go up and down in cycles. At least that's what history shows us. There are good times and bad times; periods of boom followed by bust and recession.

The stock market anticipates the future, so when people put money into shares it is because they expect the companies they are investing in to increase their profits, hence they expect the outlook for the economy to be buoyant. Billionaire trader George Soros very convincingly argues that the stock market not only anticipates the future but actually affects the outcome. So you could say that economic cycles are influenced by human mass psychology. When we are happy and optimistic about the future, we see everything in a positive light and tend to spend much more and keep splurging. This pushes the stock market higher, we feel even wealthier, and then start to borrow money. This usually creates a debt spiral, as we borrow more and more until something happens that acts as a catalyst to change the mass mood. When we fear what the future holds and our confidence vanishes, we pull our belts in and slow right down on the spending front. In this scenario, the world seems to be coming to an end. This negative sentiment is reflected in the sluggish economy, and is otherwise known as a recession (see Bear Market, Boom/Bust, Bull Market, Kondratieff Cycle).

Cyclical Shares

These are shares that are very sensitive to changes in the economic cycle. When times are good they flourish and when times are bad they suffer adversely. Examples are building companies, manufacturers and luxury goods makers. Lots of investors try to outsmart the market by watching these shares to try to guess when the next economic upturn or downturn is coming. This is a pretty risky way to make decisions about investing in shares. For one thing, the market can and does get it wrong. So it's better to buy shares that have a convincing story over the long haul, and which are not subject to the vagaries of fashion, whim or market sentiment (see Defensive Shares).

Dawn Raid

Rather confusingly, dawn raids can occur at tea-time as well, which is a much more civilized time to conduct one of these, if you ask me. In City terms, this occurs when someone keen to get hold of a large chunk of a company's shares, often with a view to making a bid for the whole company, dives in and buys up as many shares as he or she can in one fell swoop, rather than trying to stealthily and quietly build up a stake in the company over a period of weeks. The element of surprise is the key here. Anyone can buy a sizeable slug of a company's shares without having to declare it to the Stock Exchange. Beyond a certain percentage the buyer has to inform the Takeover Panel (see City Code, Takeover Panel).

There are a couple of less jolly interpretations of this phrase. It can be when HM Revenue & Customs sends a swarm of its tax inspectors to investigate a business it suspects of tax fraud. And just occasionally, the UK Serious Fraud Office storms the epicentre of the Square Mile and claps handcuffs on naughty boys and girls who have done wrong.

Day Trader

Day traders are private individuals like you and me, who want to make big dosh and aren't prepared to wait around for it. Impatient with the idea of a steady career path, they've probably jacked in a good job, with the express intention of making themselves a fortune as quickly as possible. How do they try to do this? Well, they act as principal, ie, buying and selling shares on their own account in the space of a few minutes, hours or days. Day traders are a relatively new phenomenon, seen mainly in the United States. About 70 per cent of these guys lose serious money and only a small handful of them make anything at all. What do you call a day trader who quit with £20m? Someone who started with £50m. I suspect you've gathered that it's not a good idea to do this! (See Principal, Trader, Trading.)

Dead Cat Bounce

It is the charming phrase that City dealers use when the stock market plummets downwards and then pathetically bounces a tiny bit, only to sink flat on its back again.

Dealing

Nothing seedy like drugs or dope, man. This merely describes the act of buying or selling shares. The people who are instructed to do the actual buying or selling are called dealers. They go into the market (metaphorically speaking, because all share dealing is now done over the telephone or by computer with the help of screens that display all the various prices on offer) and buy or sell shares at the best prevailing price at the time of dealing. Then they report the trade, or 'bargain', back to the stockbroker or fund manager who placed the order.

Debenture

A business has a wide choice in the way it raises money. Selling shares in the business is one way. Another way is to borrow cash. A debenture is like a mortgage, only instead of you grovelling to the building society for a long-term loan, it's a company grovelling to you. Just as you have to offer your house as collateral to the building society if anything should go wrong, so a business offers you its fixed assets in the shape of land or buildings, etc, which act as collateral against the debenture money you're lending them. In the same way that you have to pay the building society interest for the privilege of borrowing money from it, so a company pays you interest for getting its mitts on your cash. Debentures can also be bonds. They are one of the more solid, safe types of loan you can make to a company in the world of finance (see AAA, Bonds, Credit Rating).

Debtors

Goodie. People who actually owe you money for a change. For a company or a business, debtors are the people who owe them money.

Defensive Shares

These are shares that are perceived by investors to be immune from nasty, horrible things like recessions. Totally the opposite to cyclical shares, they are better equipped (allegedly) to weather stormy economic weather. What sort of shares are these? Well, food, drugs and healthcare are obvious examples. No matter what happens, we still need to eat, drink and take drugs, not the recreational variety, I hasten to add! The thing to be wary of is that whilst these types of shares all fall under the same umbrella of safe and defensive, some cope better with the vagaries of a turbulent economy than others. Investors tend to pile into these when they feel the economy is about to tip into a downturn and they want to batten down the hatches, investment-wise (see Cyclical Shares, Utility Shares).

Deferred Shares

Occasionally a company issues shares in which the dividend payment is deferred until some point in the future. Things like voting rights can also be deferred. These shares will be cheaper than the ordinary version to reflect the disadvantages of owning them. When they are no longer deferred, the price of the shares will rise to reflect that. There can be tax advantages in owning shares where the income stream, ie, dividends, is not received until some future date, thus delaying the need to pay tax on your dividend income.

Defined Benefits Scheme

A long-winded way of saying final salary pension (see Pension – Final Salary Pension).

Defined Contributions Scheme

A long-winded way of saying money purchase pension (see Pension – Money Purchase Pension).

Deflation

The opposite of inflation, where wages and prices keep going up. Instead, wages and prices fall. Economists wail that falling prices are just as corrosive and bad for the economy as rising prices. They say deflation is usually a disaster for the 'man in the street'. The reason? A company would argue, 'Why should we employ someone to make a car that we can only sell in the future for 90 per cent of the cost of making it today?' So deflation can bring mass unemployment and only people with lots of cash benefit from this scenario.

Dematerialized Shareholding

Oh no, my shares in Star Fleet plc have dematerialized! Now I'll never get them back. Relax. They haven't evaporated into thin air. In the good old days, the only proof of share ownership that people had was a physical share certificate, a bit of paper that said, for example, that you owned 500 shares in Star Fleet plc. The up-to-date way of storing them is in an electronic system called CREST (see CREST). The good news is that for all of you fretting that you might forget about your shares, or worse still, they might evaporate, indeed, dematerialize, you can still ask your stockbroker for a share certificate when you buy them.

Demerger

It's when a company sells off a part of its business. There are several reasons why it might do this. Maybe to raise cash for the parent company, or perhaps to enhance shareholder value because the individual parts of the business are worth more than the whole. Another reason for chopping off a part of itself is if there is no synergy between the bit being jettisoned and the core business.

What actually happens is that the single company splits into two entities, which then lead two separate existences. Shareholders in the original single company should typically get proportionate shares in each of the new enterprises.

Demutualization

By now a fair few of you have received cash windfalls as a result of demutualizations, so you probably know what it is. It is when a financial organization that is owned and run purely for the benefit of its members, such as a building society, is transformed into a bank, which is floated on the Stock Exchange and is then owned by its shareholders, who may or may not be beneficiaries of its services.

Deposit Account

This is where you deposit money into a bank or building society and expect to leave it there for a longish length of time in the hope of getting better interest than if it stays languishing in your current account earning diddly rates of interest. A good way of finding out who is offering the most attractive rates of interest is to visit the Moneyfacts website, which is used by professional advisers and will tell you everything on offer by the whole gamut of financial institutions: www.moneyfacts.co.uk.

Depositary Receipts

There are lots of companies that want to gain access to international investors who might otherwise be put off by the tricky conditions of the local stock market in which the shares are listed. How do they get round this? Here's an example. A Korean power company wants to gain access to the global share market to raise funds. It is difficult for foreign investors to buy and sell shares in the local Korean stock market. Solution? The Korean company creates a large chunk of its own shares that it then hands over to an investment bank whose job it is to make those shares internationally marketable. The bank creates a subsidiary that transforms those locally traded shares into depositary shares or receipts. There are various ways it can do this, but it might package 50 locally traded shares into one depositary share for example. These are then issued and traded on a major stock market, such as that of the United States or the United Kingdom. The point about these is that they offer investors an uncomplicated way of participating in more obscure or exotic stock markets. They have their own dynamic and often trade at a premium to the locally traded shares in the same company, simply because investors prefer the easy route of being able to buy shares in, say, KEPCO (Korea Electricity Power Company) in a mainstream stock market. Depositary shares can be American or Global, depending on how they are structured when they are created (see American Depositary Receipts – ADR).

Depreciation

What exactly is it? Well, when you buy a brand new car, it pretty much loses a large chunk of its value as soon as it leaves the showroom (unless it's a very fancy, scarce, limited-edition Jag – sigh!). In the same way, when a company buys tangible things for its business, like computers, they're worth less and less, ie, lose value, over time. These falls in value are accounted for in a company's accounts by way of depreciation. A simple example: if a company has bought a machine that makes squidgets for £100,000 and this squidget-making machine is expected to last for ten years, then the company spreads the cost of the machine evenly over ten years in its accounts (see Amortization, Tangible Assets). Currencies, too, can depreciate. When inflation erodes the value of the local currency it is called domestic depreciation.

Derivatives – Options, Contracts For Difference, Futures, Warrants

What *is* a derivative? Surprise! Derivatives derive from something. They are bits of paper, just like shares. They derive from things like shares, bonds, commodities, etc.

A derivative is basically a contract between two people to buy or sell an asset (it could be shares, gold, pork bellies, etc) in the future at a price fixed now. It derives from things like shares, gold, etc, and its price is linked to the price of the underlying financial instrument. Different derivatives are traded in different ways. They can allow investors to gear up, ie, put up a small amount of money to gain exposure to a much bigger slice of the action. In theory you can make large profits on a small outlay, but the reality is that it is similar to having a flutter on the horses. There are only a few types of derivative. Once we cut through the jargon, they are straightforward. Here are the main ones:

Options

Why use options? Suppose you think a share is going to go up or down and you want to make money on that idea. But you do not want to put much money into it. Options allow you to put a bet on your idea. If you get it wrong, you will only lose the amount of money you put upfront. If you get it right, you make a nice profit. There are two types of options – traditional and traded:

Traditional Options

Let's say you like the look of Vodafone shares. You believe they are going to go through the roof in the next few months. However, you do not want to spend a large amount of money buying the shares in case you are wrong. You could buy a 'call' option in them. This gives you the right, but not the obligation, to buy Vodafone shares at a fixed price and within a defined period of time in the future. You pay a 'premium' to buy the 'call' just as you might pay an insurance premium. In a worst case scenario, if the shares fall out of bed (City-speak for going down sharply!) you do not have to take up your option. You can let it lapse and the only money you lose is the 'call' money or 'premium'. The opposite of a 'call' is a 'put' option. This gives you the right, but not the obligation, to sell shares at a fixed price sometime in the future.

Buying traditional options is not so bad on the risk front, because you only stand to lose the money paid up for them in the first place. However, they are not tradable. This type of option is available in a large variety of shares. It can also be used to 'hedge': suppose you own a large holding of GlaxoSmithKline shares. You are worried that the stock market is going to fall sharply. You could buy a 'put' option to lock in the prevailing high price of those shares. This is known as 'hedging'. If you are correct and the shares do drop sharply, you have the right to sell your shares at the high price you fixed several months ago. Rather like a punt on the gee-gees, though, these options can often turn out to be useless!

Traded Options

Exactly the same as traditional options but with one important difference. You can buy and sell the options themselves, just like shares. The choice of these is limited to a handful of very widely traded major shares. But the same principles apply. If you get it wrong buying these, you will still only lose your initial outlay of money. The added frisson of excitement comes from making money with them if your idea goes right.

How do you buy and sell options? You call a stockbroker who deals in options. He buys the option for you from an options trader who 'writes' the option and is effectively like a bookmaker (see Writer). The options trader takes a view and offers odds to the punter (you).

Contracts For Difference – CFD

These are another type of derivative. Basically a CFD is a contract between two people who agree to settle the difference (plus or minus) on an underlying asset at some time in the future. With these you are betting on the movement of the price of a share rather than the share itself. CFDs allow you to mirror the performance of the underlying share without actually owning them. They are structured so you can trade them on 'margin', which means investors only pay a relatively small amount of money in order to own a much larger chunk of the shares. The risks and rewards are high and these, just like futures and spread betting, are categorically not for anyone who's green around the gills when it comes to investing. Here's an example: you pay £10,000 to own £100,000 worth of Bloggins plc shares. If things go well and the shares rocket, you're singing 'We're in the money' and quaffing champagne. If the company goes bust you are committed to pay out the full £100,000. Ugh!

At the moment, the vast majority of CFDs traded apply to UK and US shares. They are becoming more and more popular with investors because they are cheaper and more flexible than getting into options. Another advantage of CFDs is that the folks who trade in these don't have to pay stamp duty on any purchases (see Financial Services Authority, Margin, Margin Call, Risk/Reward Ratio, Spread Betting, Tax – Stamp Duty).

CFDs are not technically the same as options, but similar in that you can make money from falling share prices as well as rising ones. Unlike options you do qualify for any dividends paid. Fund managers are increasingly starting to use them to hedge shares they own as well as ones they don't (see Hedging, Short).

Futures

These are the wonder toys of the financial markets. What is a 'future'? The purchaser of a futures contract commits himself to take delivery of or deliver a fixed quantity of a commodity, currency, etc, at a fixed price on some future date. The futures contract is tradable, ie, the owner can offload it on to someone else if he so chooses. Why a futures contract is so dangerous is that for a relatively small outlay of cash upfront, it commits the owner to a potentially unlimited loss if the market goes against him, because he has to honour the contract regardless. The only way to wriggle out of this obligation is if the owner of the futures contract sells it on to some other mug who thinks he is the mug and buys it from him. Otherwise, when the contract expires, the lucky owner will get physical delivery of 1 ton of oil or soya beans!

Firms can use futures to lower, or hedge risk. Example: your bacon factory needs a regular supply of pork bellies over the whole year. Problem is, the price of pork bellies changes depending on supply. Solution: you fix the price now at which you will pay for pork bellies in the future. This guarantees your future supply of them, the price you will pay and hopefully irons out the highs and lows of pork belly prices during the year.

Nowadays, futures are being used more and more by speculators, who, just like our home-grown Nick Leeson, think they know better than anyone else what the future moves of a stock market, commodity, currency, etc will be. This use of futures increasingly affects stock market movements, hence the value of your pension or share portfolio.

Play with futures and you are either deranged, drunk or seriously rich! If you are even contemplating 'investing' in them (author snorts with derision), take two aspirin and lie down (see Euronext LIFFE).

Warrants

The more cynical might think there ought to be a lot more of these issued for the arrest of nefarious City types. Warrants, though, are just bits of paper that give you a long-term option to buy shares in a company at a fixed date and price in the future. They are different from options in that they usually have a lifespan of a number of years, whereas options only last for months. You can buy and sell warrants just like shares.

Covered Warrants

The principle behind covered warrants is just the same as for options and warrants, ie, for a small outlay of cash you can 'gear up'. By buying these you have the right, but not the obligation, to buy or sell securities at a fixed price on or before a future date. They are usually used by investors who want to 'hedge', ie, protect what they already own, and apply to a broader range of financial instruments than just shares. You can buy these for indices, commodities, currencies, a basket of shares, etc. They are listed on the London Stock Exchange, therefore are actually tradable in their own right and settled in the same way as ordinary shares. Unlike options and warrants, however, these cannot be sold 'short', ie, you have to have bought a covered warrant before you can sell it. This makes them less risky than traded options, contracts for difference and futures. They also differ from options in that they have a longer lifespan, generally 3–24 months, as opposed to an option's life, which is usually 3–9 months.

Note: for any of the above sophisticated investments, if you are deemed as a 'private client' you are entitled to compensation if you are mis-sold or given bad advice on them. Anyone deemed to be an 'expert client' by the regulatory authority (ie, someone who already knows what he or she is doing) is not entitled to any compensation if things go horribly wrong.

Designated Account

See Nominee Account.

Devaluation

Devaluation is the word that describes the lowering of the value of one currency against other currencies. This can happen either because the traders in the currency markets reckon that the currency is overvalued, or because the government, for economic reasons, wants to make its currency cheaper. History shows that governments always seem to orchestrate a devaluation to get their country out of trouble. A devaluation is often accompanied by the country's central bank printing lots of extra money, which is pushed into the financial system to avert a credit crunch and businesses going bust (see Central Bank, Inflation). This is not good news for the economy, as it is highly inflationary. The corollary to printing lots of notes is that each unit of the currency is worth less, and so devaluation is a logical word to describe it, isn't it?

Dictum Meum Pactum

Something that seems to be ever rarer in the smooth-talking financial world. Latin for 'My word is my bond', this was the City's *modus operandi* in the good old days. A verbal agreement and a handshake was enough to seal a deal. Giving your word used to mean something. The whole of the City operated on trust, and because it was a comparatively small 'club', anyone who welched on a deal was ostracized and people would refuse to deal with him.

Today it's a different story. The City is too vast and populated with too many people to operate on such a genteel level. These days, every conversation is tape-recorded and there are swarms of lawyers and compliance officers to make sure everybody is keeping their word and being honourable and truthful. (Can you hear me quietly choking over my double decaff cappuccino?)

Dilution

You take ten lemons and squeeze them, diluting with… This is not Delia Smith's cookery book? Sorry about that folks, I must remember we are on the riveting subject of finance. Dilution might be good for Delia, but I'm afraid it's not good news in the financial sense. This can happen to a shareholder when a company issues more shares in itself by way of a rights issue. If you've got shares in that company, and you don't take up your rights, your holding, post-rights issue, will be smaller in proportion to what it used to be, ie, it will be diluted (see Rights Issue).

Discount

Did somebody say discount? Am I going to get a good deal for once in my life? Don't get too excited. This is yet more City-speak. When the stock market discounts the future, it doesn't necessarily mean that share prices are getting cheaper. Discounting is the term City folks use to describe the market's anticipation of future events. When shares rise, the market is discounting a rosy economic outlook, and when they drop, the market is discounting bad times ahead.

An alternative meaning for this word is when a share is standing at a discount to its net asset value. This means that the company has assets worth more than its total value on the Stock Exchange (see Investment Trust, Net Asset Value per Share).

Discount Broker

This phrase has two meanings. For most of us it describes the bare essentials, no-frills dealing service offered by stockbrokers to those of us who know exactly what shares we want to buy and sell. They do the bargains (transactions) at a bargain! (See Execution Only.)

The other use for this term is when discount brokers, operating from discount houses, sell bits of paper called bills that are effectively IOUs. They are issued by companies needing to borrow large sums of cash for a short period of time, such as six months. The bills (similar to, but not the same as bonds) offer a fixed income stream and are also known as short-term promissory notes. The reason why the word discount features so prominently in this context is that the bills are offered at a discount to their actual value, which acts as an incentive to persuade lenders to part with their cash. There is a whole market out there for short-term company paper, and these types of investments are predominantly bought and sold by the big players, ie, the institutions. They are not so suitable for the individual investor.

Discounted Cash Flow

This is the complicated mathematical calculation that works out the value today of money received tomorrow. Let me enlighten you – one pound in the hand now is worth more than two in the bush later, or am I mixing my metaphors? Anyhow, the reason why City folks like to do this calculation is because they argue that money received in the future won't be worth as much as it is now. Why? The usual arguments: inflation erodes the value of money and if you had it in your sweaty palm now, you could pop it into the building society and it would be earning interest this very minute. Of course, if you had the money in your hand now, you would be absolutely certain of receiving it! (See Present Value of Money.)

Discount House

A company that buys bills at a discount (see Discount Broker). Only a few discount houses qualify to be an 'accepting house', the term that describes an old-fashioned club of companies that were given regulatory approval to borrow money at reduced rates of interest.

Discretionary – Dealing, Portfolio Management

Basically when you hand your money to stockbrokers or fund managers on a discretionary basis, you are effectively giving them total control to do with it what they see fit. They have free rein to invest it in shares, bonds, etc and de-invest from shares, or whatever. To trust someone to that extent, you should be absolutely certain that they have an ace track record. Be sure in your own mind that these people are competent and up to the job. Discuss with them at great length what you want to achieve and the level of risk you are willing to take on, or you could end up wishing you'd left your money in the boringly dull, but safe building society deposit account! (See Association of Private Client Investment Managers, Churning, Stockbroker.)

Disinflation

Inflation is when prices rise. Deflation is when prices fall. Disinflation is when the actual rate of price rises slows down. This is the government's favourite scenario. As soon as they feel inflation is getting out of control, they implement deflationary measures (like raising interest rates or increasing taxation) in order to achieve disinflation (see Fiscal Policy, Monetary Policy).

Distribution Funds

Often collective funds are marketed as being specialized in one area, such as 'growth' or 'income' to suit the different needs of investors. 'Distribution' funds invest in shares and bonds with a view to delivering to investors a combination of both these elements, ie, 'growth' and 'income', in one (see Active Management, Collective Funds, Growth Funds, Income Funds, Investment Trust, Managed Funds, Unit Trust).

Diversification

In financial terms, diversification is spreading money over a wide range of assets. You probably already instinctively know the reason why people diversify. They do it to spread risk, ie, lessen the chances of losing all their money in one hit by not putting their proverbial eggs into one basket. Obviously the more money you have, the easier it gets to diversify. Many people like to entrust their savings with the bods, ie, the institutions that are professionally paid to manage the collective savings of lots of individuals like us (see Asset Allocation, Managed Funds). It's much harder for us to spread our money as widely as they do. But before you get too despondent, cheer up. You, too, can diversify your assets in your own way. Big items generally take precedence, so it's obviously a good thing to own a place of your own to rest your tired head. And then spare cash should be spread over a handful of assets, some into shares, some into unit trusts, maybe some antiques, etc. And of course, always have some emergency money put away for the unwelcome event of a horrible mishap.

Dividend

The money a company pays out to its shareholders from the profits it has made. If you've got shares in British Gas or whatever, you'll receive a dividend cheque (most likely two per year – an interim dividend and a final one). With the cheque comes an innocuous little detachable slip called a tax voucher that you need to file away neatly for that joyous time when you do your tax return (see Tax Return).

Dividend Cover

Anything with cover in the phrase means 'How safe is it?' Dividend cover checks out how many times over a company could pay out its dividend all at once, if it chose to do so. It is a terribly easy calculation that City bods do to ascertain just how safe the future dividend payout is:

$$\frac{\text{Earnings}}{\text{Gross Dividend Paid}} = \text{Dividend Cover}$$

Obviously the higher the number, the more secure the dividend payout to shareholders. If the dividend isn't covered, then shareholders had better start worrying.

Dividend Yield

You arrive at this by yet another terribly easy calculation:

$$\frac{\text{Gross Dividend Paid per Share}}{\text{Current Share Price}} \times 100 = \text{Dividend Yield}$$

By now you know that yield is simply the return you get for your original outlay of cash into something, whether it is shares or any other type of investment. So what's so special about the dividend? Well, apart from profits, the dividend is another key indicator that shows how well a company is doing. In general, dividends tend to rise when a company is doing well and vice versa. Numbers like these are much simpler to follow for larger companies, because they are easier to predict. Get into smaller companies and the outlook is much more uncertain, and returns are more volatile. City analysts get absorbed in 'divi' yield because it gives an indication of the returns investors are likely to get in the future when they invest their money in the shares of a particular company.

The historical dividend yield (based on what the company has paid out in the past) is just an indication of what it may pay in the future. It doesn't guarantee anything. As City folks set great store by what the future holds, they obviously do their utmost to do the whole crystal ball thing and predict what the dividend will be next time round (called the prospective dividend yield). When they get it right, they pat themselves vigorously on the back, and when they get it wrong, naturally it was the company's fault, as they didn't give the analyst enough information to go on! Incidentally, a low dividend doesn't necessarily mean that there is a problem if a company is making loads of juicy profits and reinvesting these in lucrative areas of business. Rather perversely, a high dividend can mean that a company is in trouble (see Growth Shares, High-Yield Shares, Yield).

Dog

A dog is a dud share. It is usually the share that a good 'friend' tipped you to buy. Admit it, we all fall for the oldest trick in the book, which is invariably, that by the time someone is tipping a share to us, the rest of the world is piling out of them. The dog has been sitting in your portfolio for years, and you've always refused to sell it in the conviction that one day, it will rise in value. And very occasionally, luck strikes and it does. The lovely City expression – every dog has its day – describes the sheer luck of seeing the worst performing share in your portfolio resurrected, like Lazarus. What could catalyse this? Well, if a share performs diabolically for long enough, a predator might come out of the woodwork and gobble it up. If you're unlucky, though, the dog could equally exhibit rigor mortis and throw all four paws in the air!

Dow Jones 500 – DJ 500

This is an index that tracks the fortunes of America's 500 largest companies and it is a good barometer of the overall US economy, certainly more so than the Dow Jones Industrial Average. Since the American stock market is the most important in the world, all eyes in the City are firmly fixed on it every day. Our own UK stock market is much smaller in comparison, but it is still the fifth largest one in the world after the United States, France, Germany and Japan (see Dow Jones Industrial Average – DJIA, Footsie – FTSE 100, Index).

Dow Jones Industrial Average – DJIA

The DJIA follows the fortunes of 30 top American industrial companies, with world-famous names such as IBM and Coca Cola. Although they are not necessarily the largest companies by value (Bill Gates's Microsoft is actually on NASDAQ: see NASDAQ), it is the index all eyes turn to when trying to guess the future. 'Did you see the Dow today? Up 30 points. Do you think it's going to crash?' 'Naah. Going to the moon, it is.' Oft-repeated conversation between two wide-boy traders trying to guess what the long term holds (which for them is the next five minutes!).

Drip Feeding

Something you'll need when you collapse in horror at realizing how much money you've lost in emerging markets. The true City version is the sensible policy of dripping your money into markets, unit trusts, or whatever little by little. Sort of toe-in-the-water strategy. If you get a headache at the mere thought of putting your hard-earned cash into stocks and shares, this approach to investing makes life easy for you as all it requires is that you pop a small amount of money, say £50–100 a month into a fund or funds of your choice over a long period of time. It is a sensible strategy for those people who simply cannot watch the markets closely enough to make sound judgements about market timing, ie, when to get in and when to get out. Look on the bright side: if the markets keep plunging, the money paid in will be buying more on each downward leg. Of course it all balances out, because in a rising market, it buys less (see Regular Savings Plan).

Dual Capacity

This is when a City firm has more than one function (see Single Capacity). For example, it can be an agency stockbroker, dealing on behalf of its clients, as well as acting as a market-maker, which means buying and selling shares for its own account or acting as 'principal' (see Principal). As the firm is not acting purely as an agent for its clients, but buys and sells shares for its own 'book', a potential conflict of interest could arise. An example: a client comes along and wants to buy some shares. The dual capacity firm has loads of Beeswax plc shares on its books. It doesn't take a genius to work out which shares might be recommended to the client and where they could come from. Naturally these firms vigorously protest in horror at the merest suggestion that any improper dealings ever take place. We've got Chinese walls they cry (see Chinese Walls), no way will there be any conflict of interest. Hmmm.

Due Diligence

When one company is mulling over the possibility of buying another company, it obviously has to check over all the aspects of the potential target, especially its finances. So it appoints an investment bank's corporate finance department to do all the gruelling hard work of checking the target out thoroughly to make sure there are no nasty glitches or surprises. Due diligence includes working with outside lawyers and accountants to make sure that the target's accounts and actual business are what they purport to be (see Corporate Finance, Investment Bank, Mergers & Acquisitions).

E

EAR – Equivalent Annual Rate

Applies specifically to overdrafts and shows the compounded annual cost of the loan expressed as a percentage. It does not take into account any additional charges (eg, penalty fees) that may be applicable (see Compounding).

Earnings per Share – EPS

You can wake up now as we've reached one of the really crucial numbers that is worth noting. Earnings per share, or eps, is a mathematical calculation that takes a company's net profits and divides it by the total number of the company's shares in issue. The calculation establishes how much profit is available to each individual share of the company and is normally shown in pence. Taken in isolation, the number doesn't mean very much. It becomes more meaningful when seen in context over a period of a few years. Looking at the eps over the last five years can give you a very good idea of whether a company's earnings are growing, falling, or whether there was a temporary (or permanent) blip in profits. It is also useful in comparing one share with another, provided they are in the same industry sector. Earnings per share is one of the most vitally important measures investors use to decide whether they're going to bite the bullet and invest their money in a company or not (see Corporate Earnings Growth, Price/Earnings Ratio, Price/EBITDA Ratio).

Earnings Yield

Yield is simply the return you get on the cash you invested. Earnings yield is the earnings per share of a company expressed as a percentage of the cost of each share in that company. It's worked out by a slightly complicated mathematical equation that you needn't bother with, and is usually higher than the dividend yield of a share. Why do investors want to know this number? Because it demonstrates how profitable a company is compared with the cost of buying its shares (see Dividend Yield, Earnings per Share, Yield).

Economist

A person who portentously studies and predicts the future of the state of our economy, the US economy, and any other economy that takes his or her fancy. Those that are gainfully (some might say ungainfully!) employed by the City are handsomely rewarded for their predictions. And the beauty of what they do, ie, forecast the future, is that it doesn't matter a hoot if they get it wrong! In this scenario, they simply make the necessary alterations to their previous forecasts and go with the flow. Truthfully, crystal ball gazing for the various economies around the world is a pretty thankless task. It is hard for anybody to get it spot on, even the experts.

Economy

Every country in the world has one. An economy is basically like a giant employee that earns money, and its Treasury is like the household budget, with incomings and outgoings on a massive scale. Some are more prosperous than others (see Fiscal Policy, Monetary Policy).

Efficient Market Theory

There are those who argue that it's useless to try and beat the stock market because share prices always reflect all relevant known information at any given time (see Random Walk Theory). The theory assumes that if information circulates freely and shares can be easily traded, then the market will operate efficiently, with supply and demand determining share prices. Nice theory. Pity it doesn't seem to work!

Emerging Markets

This is the general term describing stock markets belonging to countries that, either for political or economic reasons, have not yet taken part on the world financial stage. Examples are the 'tiger' markets dotted around South-East Asia. Just like small companies, emerging stock markets react very strongly when investors pour large amounts of money into these tiny stock exchanges, thus forcing the prices of their small, illiquid companies sky-high. When the love affair is over, these same international big guys withdraw their money with equal vigour, and the erstwhile glamorous emerging markets are brutally dumped. In the bid to make investing in these countries seem more attractive, 'emerging' conveys the impression that they are hip and exciting places to put your hard-earned cash. That is, until they nosedive.

It is helpful if the brokers enthusing about these markets remember to place a high-risk tag on this type of investment. All too often, they get carried away in the euphoria of the moment. Russia is a good example. Only in 1998 the Russian market was up 100 per cent – 'going to the moon'. Golly, were Russian bonds popular, just before Russia decided to default on its debt! Oops. Unfortunately the market retraced all its progress as the country teetered for a while on bankruptcy. The key thing to remember with emerging markets is, HIGH RISK, HIGH REWARD (see Risk/Reward Ratio).

Employee Share Option Plan – ESOP

There are those fortunate enough to work for a company that's going places that gives its staff the opportunity to buy its shares. The company usually makes an offer too good to refuse, like one free share for every share the employee buys. Obviously the idea is that the employee should be incentivized to work with gusto and enthusiasm for the owner of the business, so they are usually obliged to hang on to the shares for a minimum period of time, after which they can sell them if they choose to. An ESOP is when the employee puts aside a small amount of money every month into a savings scheme to buy shares. Sometimes the employer contributes to this scheme.

There are other similar schemes that allow employees to buy shares in the company they work for. Save As You Earn is the most commonly used (see Save As You Earn, Share Options).

Endowment

An endowment is a life insurance policy that is invested into an investment fund. If you have one of these, in theory, you should get back a lump sum of money that has grown much larger over its lifetime (usually 10–25 years). The idea is that the insurance company you have the policy with will invest it wisely for you on your behalf. The good news is that they cough up whether or not you die – how considerate! The glitches though, are that they are expensive and inflexible. If the investment is not held for the whole duration (10–30 years) you can get badly penalized and there has been a lot of bad press surrounding this.

With-profits endowments are the most common variety. Every year they should grow in value because of the cumulative effect of yearly bonuses. There's also a terminal bonus as the policy expires, though hopefully you won't! Typically, there is a catch. The final bonus is not guaranteed by any means. If the company's investments perform abysmally you won't get anything at all. Annual bonuses are guaranteed to continue even if you stop adding premiums to an endowment. Some people sell their endowment policies to raise cash. For this they need to consult a specialist in second-hand endowment sales (see With-Profits Policy).

Enterprise Investment Scheme – EIS

These are investments in small companies with assets no bigger than £15m for which the government gives you very generous tax breaks. Companies this small are usually held in private hands, ie, unquoted, or listed on the junior stock markets, such as OFEX and AIM. For those fortunate enough to have made loads of money on the sale of something that is liable to capital gains tax, if that money goes straight into an EIS, the payment of that tax is deferred. The catch with the tax breaks (and have you ever known the government to give away anything?) is that you have to keep your money in the investment for three years. This is an area needing specialist advice as these investments are higher risk than more plain vanilla ones. Of course that means the rewards can be higher, too (see Tax – Capital Gains Tax, Deferred Tax).

Equity

Not the trade union for luvvies. In business and City-speak, when you own a stake in anything, be it land, property or a business, you own equity. 'Equities' is the general term used to describe ordinary shares in a company (see Shares).

Equity Release

This is a way of releasing value in your home, particularly as people get older, in order to supplement any pension income. The idea behind it is to pre-sell part of your property while you're still alive so as to get an income from it. For those considering these schemes, the key is to fully understand what you're getting into and all the costs associated with them, as these can be extremely high (see Home Income Plan).

Escrow

When two people are squabbling over money and who it belongs to (what's new?), and the money that's being argued over is held in the safe hands of an independent third party, it is in an escrow account. Most often a lawyer sets up the escrow account.

Ethical Investments/Funds

Are you a keen smoker, drinker, gambler and fervent believer in the usefulness of pollution? Then perhaps ethical investing isn't for you! As the term implies, it is the conscious choice of people to invest their money into investments such as shares or funds holding shares of companies that they deem to be ethically run, ie, they only put their money into ventures or funds that uphold certain moral criteria. So companies that make nasty things that kill people, such as armaments, ciggies or booze, are a no-no. Animal testing is also out. Alternatively, good things that help keep the environment clean, like manufacturers of catalytic converters (the gadgets that convert pollutant gases into less harmful ones), and things that save lives and products that help others (you get the picture) are deemed ethical. This is an increasingly popular strand of investment as people become ever more eco-friendly. For more info on ethical funds contact EIRIS, www.eiris.org.

Euro

This is the name given to the single currency that has replaced the various European currencies, such as the French franc, German mark and Irish punt. So far 11 countries have elected to be a part of the European Monetary Union or EMU. Their Central Banks will probably vanish, to be replaced by the European Central Bank. Britain (to date) has assiduously avoided participation. (See European Monetary Union, European Union.)

Eurobonds

These are bonds issued by companies in a European currency that is different from the currency of the country in which the company is based. They are issued on the Euromarket (see Euromarket below) and are not very easy for small private investors to get hold of. Often in bearer form, they are valuable, like bank notes, hence anonymous (see Bearer Securities).

Euromarket

It's not really a market and it's not European. It would be hard to find a more misleading word! It refers to securities (see Securities) that are issued and held outside their country of origin. Examples include UK sterling bonds held by investors in the United States, or Japanese yen on deposit in France.

Euronext LIFFE

The people at Euronext LIFFE are trading in the future. They buy and sell contracts that commit the owner to buy or sell a large quantity of a commodity, share index or some other financial instrument at some future date. This is unbelievably risky stuff, and for normal everyday folk, a complete no-no (see my edifying piece on Derivatives – Futures). It was one of the last open outcry financial markets in the United Kingdom, as depicted by those manic-looking barrow boys in brightly striped blazers behaving very badly and petulantly throwing bits of paper around. This has now been replaced by computerized electronic trading – boring! For more information on this ridiculously risky market, check out its website: www.euronext.com.

European Monetary Union – EMU

This describes the merger of all the European currencies into one currency Europe-wide called the euro. So far, the United Kingdom has not yet decided whether to join the party. Joining the EMU has far-reaching consequences: no more British pound, no more independent Bank of England. In theory, it's a good thing to belong to this: benefits include belonging to a powerful single market and easier cross-border trading conditions. The same advantages apply to businesses as well as individuals. But to quote Orwell, 'All animals are equal. Some animals are more equal than others'. At the time of writing it is hard to envisage how several countries with quite different economic prospects and profiles can all be squeezed comfortably under the aegis of one currency and a 'one-size-fits-all' interest rate policy (see Euro, European Union).

European Union – EU

This is the ongoing process of merging all elected European Union members under one umbrella, like the United States of America. Power in the EU is shared by the Council of Ministers (representatives of all Member States), the European Commission (which was a civil service, but now sees itself as a government) and the Parliament, whose members are directly elected, but with modest powers. The latter are called Members of European Parliament, or MEPs for short. The European Commission, based in Brussels, along with the Council of Ministers and MEPs, is making decisions on the harmonization of taxes, economic and social policy, even defence and foreign policy. The MEPs argue with the Commission and the Council of Ministers as to who should make all the decisions about really crucial stuff, you know, like the standard size of bread rolls and the height of chandeliers suspended from ceilings. There are worries that the EU seems intent on centralizing power, which could lead to much more bureaucracy in the future (see Euro, European Monetary Union).

Ex-All

Ex-all means that any buyer of shares, when they are quoted 'xa', is not entitled to receive the dividend, rights or any other things that have simultaneously just been announced (see Cum-Rights).

Ex-Capitalization

When you buy shares that are quoted ex-capitalization, it means you are not entitled to get the freebie shares (called capitalization or bonus shares) that the company has just issued to its existing shareholders. The financial press symbolize the term as 'xc', which is to be found next to the printed share price details (see Bonus Issue, Cum-Capitalization).

Exceptional Profit/Loss

This item appears in the profit and loss statement of a company's accounts. It is a one-off exceptionally large profit or loss that stems from the company's everyday business. It is shown before the tax line because the government wants to tax the profit, and is included in the company's 'operating profit'. However, to highlight the fact that it isn't likely to happen again, it is shown as a separate item (see Extraordinary Profit/Loss, Accounts).

Exchange Traded Funds – ETF

These are basically just the same as tracker funds, only with one key difference. They are actually quoted as shares; this means you can actually buy and sell ETFs on the stock market and benefit from 'real-time' pricing. They are a very cost-effective way of gaining exposure to various stock markets as you are effectively buying into one or more 'tracker' funds. A fly in the ointment is that you often have to pay an extra charge to hold these within an ISA. Barclays Bank is currently the undisputed market leader in these financial instruments, offering by far the biggest range of ETFs that cover several worldwide indices via its iShare range. Check out its website: www.iShares.net (see Diversification, Index, Individual Savings Account – ISA, Real-Time, Tracker Funds).

Ex-Dividend

When you buy shares that have gone 'ex-dividend' you are not entitled to receive the forthcoming dividend payment that the company is about to make. The financial press symbolize the term as 'xd' and it is found next to the printed share price details (see Cum-Dividend).

Execution Only

Sounds a bit violent, but it isn't! This is basically for those of you who know exactly which shares you want to buy or sell, and for how much. You ring up your stockbroker or just go on to the internet and say, 'Hi, I'm John Smith and I'd like to sell 1,000 HBOS shares at a limit of £10. Thank you very much.' And guess what? The broker goes ahead and executes the deal at the price you requested. If he can't do so, he'll get back to you and let you know, so you can alter your limit if necessary. The key is that you are in charge with this type of stockbroking service, not the broker. I like to deal in shares this way. Obviously, the less initiated will probably want advice (see Adviser – Dealing Service, Portfolio Management).

Exercise Price

Also called the strike price. In the finance world, buying an option means buying the right to buy or sell an asset at a fixed price at some point in the future. At the time of the option's purchase, the price you fix to buy or sell that asset for in the future is its 'exercise' or 'strike' price (see Derivatives – Options).

Ex-Rights

When companies need to raise more cash they can borrow money. A popular alternative is to offer investors extra shares that they can buy at a discounted price. This is called a rights issue. When this happens, obviously the original shares continue to be traded on the stock market. They usually drop in value to reflect the imminent arrival of more shares on the market, which have been sold at a lower value. Anyone who subsequently buys the shares 'ex-rights' will not be entitled to the discounted offer. It is only when the shares are sold 'cum-rights' that the new investor can take up his or her entitlement to the extra discounted shares. The financial press symbolize ex-rights as 'xr' and it's found next to the printed share price details (see Cum-Rights, Rights Issue).

Extraordinary General Meeting – EGM

When a company holds a meeting for its shareholders other than its regular, once a year Annual General Meeting (AGM) it is called an Extraordinary General Meeting or EGM. The meeting might be called because they're planning on making a big acquisition, or are themselves the target of another company. The company must consult its shareholders before deciding what to do. Shareholders vote at the meeting or in advance on a proxy form if they cannot attend (see Annual General Meeting, Proxy).

Extraordinary Profit/Loss

Like exceptional profit/loss, this pops up in a company's profit and loss account. However, it is different from an 'exceptional' item in that it is a one-off (usually large) profit or loss made by a company, which has not been incurred as part of its day-to-day activities. An example might be selling a subsidiary at a large profit. It is shown before the tax line, but after the 'operating profit' because it doesn't derive from the company's operations (see Accounts, Exceptional Profit/Loss).

F

Financial Adviser

Someone who gives you advice on your investments, including pensions and life insurance. The term financial adviser (FA) covers a wide remit – accountants, lawyers, actuaries and insurance brokers can all be FAs. When you're looking for one always check that they are properly authorized (see Financial Services Authority). Remember you're letting someone gain an intimate knowledge of your affairs, so you have to be sure you can trust them. Obviously, FAs are not altruists. They make a living out of their profession. However, when you find the right adviser, he or she can be very helpful to you. Ah, you are thinking, but how do I go about finding the right one? And how do I suss out whether they're any good or not? Read the entries for Adviser, Commission, Independent Financial Adviser, Stockbroker and Tied Financial Adviser for helpful hints.

Financial Expert

We all have a tendency to lean on other people's opinions. I know, because I regularly ask my contacts in the City to enlighten me on what is happening on the financial scene. In fact, we rely very much (perhaps too much) on people who know more than us in the world of finance. But it's not impossible to become pretty clued-up yourself. Try to find out as much as possible about the subject and take into consideration the wider scheme of things. It is important to question things, and I believe that asking the experts the right questions is half the battle. Do not get me wrong, there are many people in the financial world who are good at what they do. However, there are some who do not necessarily know a lot more than you do. Remember that investment opinions are, by their very nature, subjective. Financial expertise is mainly born of experience, which teaches us that stock market crashes are never the same each time, economic cycles never cosily repeat themselves, and heaven only knows where interest rates will be in 18 months from now. We all have an opinion on the subject and so do the experts.

One fact that we can be certain of is that the future is devilishly difficult to predict. Be aware that even the greatest experts are fallible (see Guru). So by all means, listen to what the experts are saying, and digest and process that information carefully. Then use your own counsel. Provided you exercise healthy caution and ask the right questions, then diversify your investments sensibly (see Diversification), any mistake as a result of following the advice of an expert or even just a friend won't be fatal to your financial health.

Financial Information

Information is knowledge, and in the stock market, knowledge is power. It can mean the difference between making a fortune or really losing your shirt. If you can combine the information to which you have access with good sound common sense, you have every chance of investing your money wisely and well, whether it's in the stock market or in a pension (much of which ends up being invested in the stock market anyway). The investment gurus without exception, whether they're George Soros, Peter Lynch, Warren Buffett, or even yours truly, read voraciously on their subject (see Guru). They get to know everything they can possibly know as that is what gives them the edge. They know that the more knowledge they have, the more power it gives them to make good investment decisions. 'But what do I read?' you ask with a plaintive whimper in your voice, thinking, 'Oh dear, this sounds like hard work.' I hope that by reading this book, it will give you a good kick-start into overcoming the first hurdle, the language of the money world. Here are just a few titles for absolute beginners to start dipping into:

The business section of your daily and weekend newspaper, *The Times, Daily Telegraph, Guardian, Independent, Daily Mail*, etc
Business Age
Bloomberg Money
The Economist
Financial Times
Fortune
Investor's Chronicle
Shares
Wall Street Journal

You'll also find these websites a great source of financial information:

www.citywire.co.uk
www.cnn.com
www.iii.co.uk
www.micropal.com
www.morningstar.com
www.reuters.com
www.thisismoney.co.uk

Financial Instrument

Unlike the musical variety, this just describes anything like a share, bond, currency or commodity that can be freely traded in a market or which has been used to raise money.

Financial Journalism

An important corollary to financial information (see above). There is lots of this available to the enthusiastic reader, and like the curate's egg, it's good in parts. Remember that journalists are under terrific pressure to produce lots of copy to very tight deadlines. This means they don't always get the chance to thoroughly research or fine-tune their stories. You also have to be aware that journalists usually, likely as not, have an individual bias. So check out the different slant on the same story covered in different papers. It's important to read between the lines of the financial press as it's not enough to take at face value what you are being told.

The second thing is to consider the implications of a particular news item. If the papers cover a story about instability in a tiny Middle Eastern country that just happens to be a massive oil exporter, ask yourself what will happen to the oil price. Then check what's happening to the likes of Shell and BP on the stock market, as well as companies that rely on oil supplies, such as those involved in transport and energy, etc. Bad news can sometimes give you a window of opportunity to pick up shares in a company that you've been coveting for some time, but which have stubbornly refused to fall in price. Use the newspapers as a valuable source of information to give you clues as to what is most likely to happen next or over the longer term.

Financial Manias

For some reason, every so often, lots of people get a bee in their bonnet about something or other. In France in the early nineteenth century, when the first giraffe was sent to France by Muhammad Ali of Egypt, Zarafa (Arabic for giraffe) mania took hold. People wore ridiculously high Zarafa hairstyles, got Zarafa flu and wore Zarafa ties – you get the picture. In the investment spectrum, oft-quoted examples are the South Sea Bubble and tulipomania. Do not ask me why lots of seemingly intelligent people get swept up into an irrational frenzy. It just happens. Apply this logic to stock markets, and there's a very good chance that there will be a major panic at some time in the future. It helps to try to remain a detached observer of what goes on in financial markets, so you can spot what the crowd is doing, and decide if you think that they are right or wrong. Use the mass panic, fear and greed to serve your own investment decisions.

Financial Services Authority – FSA

The all-embracing huge regulator that protects investors and the general public as far as investment business goes. It has a pretty wide remit. It makes checks on a huge variety of financial services companies. The idea is to protect in ever-greater measure the individual investor like you and me, who is more vulnerable to being ripped off than the professionals. Of course the direct consequence of all this extra policing is that these financial firms now have to spend much more on compliance (see Compliance), hence for smaller investors, the cost of getting any advice at all, let alone good advice, just keeps going up and up. Check it out at: www.fsa.gov.uk.

Financial Services Compensation Scheme

This is the last resort for people who have had bad advice or been conned by a financial services firm. Let's take the hideously nightmarish scenario that you have been cheated by dishonest fund managers to whom you entrusted your cash in the hope that they would increase it over a period of time. If the firm was authorized by the Financial Services Authority to do investment business (see above), then you may have some redress if you've already tried to get compensation from the firm and failed because they've gone bust. Contact them at: www.fscs.org.uk (see Independent Financial Adviser – IFA).

Fiscal Policy

The government decides how much it is going to extort, I mean extract, from us as far as taxes go. This is called fiscal policy. It then works out how to spend this money. Once it has cheerfully gone on a huge spending spree and realizes that there's not enough money in the kitty to carry out any other plans, like propping up the valiant National Health Service and helping the poor and needy, it then borrows money from us in the form of gilts, which is part of its monetary policy (see Gilts, Monetary Policy).

Fixed Interest

Any investment that offers you a regular fixed payment at a pre-determined rate (also known as a fixed rate of return) is known as a fixed interest security or bond. In the United Kingdom, the main bonds are gilts, company bonds and debentures (see AAA, Bonds, Corporate Bonds, Credit Rating, Debentures, Gilts, Loan Stock).

Fledgling

A young company that's just been brought on to the stock market. Usually very small in size (see AIM, Ofex).

Floating Currency

When governments give up the fruitless task of trying to control their currency's exchange rate against other currencies, it is called floating the currency. This means allowing the market to determine what the exchange rate should be. Most currencies are floating, but some are pegged to another currency. The Hong Kong dollar, for instance, is currently pegged to the US dollar.

Floating Rate Note

A banknote that you spot floating on top of a puddle and whisk away before anyone else has had time to claim it. Seriously, when companies borrow money in the form of bills, not bonds, they do so expressly to borrow for the short term. Instead of fixing the amount of money they will pay to the lender of the cash, they set criteria that offer flexibility and allow for the fact that interest rates might well fluctuate even over such a short period of time. Let's take an example: the borrower agrees to pay the lender a margin of 2 per cent more than LIBOR (the London Interbank Offered Rate). LIBOR is the interest rate at which top-quality banks are prepared to lend to each other in the short-term money markets. Consequently the rate of interest paid to the lender will always 'float' above LIBOR by 2 per cent, whether the LIBOR rate goes up or down.

Flotation

When a company's shares are sold for the first time on the stock market it is called a flotation or an IPO (Initial Public Offering, to the uninitiated!). All companies that get listed on the Stock Exchange have to be public limited companies, ie, plcs, although not all plcs are listed on the Stock Exchange.

Footsie – FTSE 100

It's an index that is pretty much regarded as the benchmark of the UK stock market. It follows the fortunes of the United Kingdom's top 100 listed companies. The FTSE 100 makes up a sizeable chunk of the total UK stock market. As the fortunes of these companies change, and they grow bigger or smaller, they are plucked out of the index or groomed for entry, and this is decided by a committee that meets every three months (see Index).

Front-End Loading

It's when you pay upfront charges for an investment product; often to pay commission to the adviser. When you buy an investment, be it a unit trust, pension or life assurance policy, you pay commission. Dear me, did you think all those salespeople selling these things are altruists who give you advice out of the kindness of their own hearts? Much of the time, their commission on flogging, I mean, advising you on your pension is given to them in your first instalment of payment(s). This is front-end loading.

So, in the case of an insurance policy or pension, if you change your mind and decide to cancel your policy within a couple of years of taking it out, you won't get much back, because most of it will have been absorbed as commission. But you can do something about this! If you ask the right questions you can get salespeople to rebate some of the commission, or spread out payments over a period of time. It means that if you change your mind and want to exit the investment, you won't take such a severe financial hit (see Commission, Independent Financial Adviser).

Front-end loading can also apply to the interest you have to pay on a mortgage or HP contract. Here you pay a high percentage of the interest on the money you've borrowed in the first period of the loan. As time goes by, interest repayments dwindle and the lion's share of the repayments becomes capital, ie, the lump sum of money lent to you (see Mortgage). Before you get too excited, though, the overall amount you pay remains the same!

Front Running

This is when a stockbroker takes advantage of any juicy 'price-sensitive' information he might be privy to, and buys or sells the shares for himself before letting his clients know. Terribly naughty, strictly forbidden and totally unethical and wrong. This probably still happens, but not as often as some curmudgeonly cynics like to think (see Inside Information, Insider Dealing).

Fundamentals/Fundamental Analysis

When a stock market crashes, City analysts tend to nod their heads sagely and remark, 'The market had lost sight of the fundamentals.' Looking at the fundamentals of a business means evaluating the quality of the assets owned by the company, its products, the outlook for those products, the efficiency with which the company is run, the quality of its management, how it compares with its competitors, the future outlook for the industry it is operating in, etc. This fundamental analysis helps to establish the true value of a business (or what the value should be) on the stock market. A real bugbear of mine is the ridiculously short-term nature of these assessments. If a company does badly in one quarter, analysts do a U-turn faster than you can say 'Fundamentals!' and yesterday's sexy, growth story can easily become a dog for years on end (see Analyst, Technical Analysis).

Fund Management

Also called asset management. People who do the job of managing the collective money of thousands of small investors are called fund managers. As fund management groups, they also manage the lolly of the huge pension and life assurance funds. In the end, though, it's all the money belonging to individuals like you and me. They are the undisputed big players in the stock markets (see Active Management, Collective Funds, Institutional Investors, Investment Trust, Managed Funds, Unit Trust).

Fund of Funds

Also called an umbrella fund, this invests its money in other funds, which in turn invest their money directly into shares, bonds and other investments. The term 'umbrella' just describes the legal framework of authorization, which encompasses all the sub-funds that it is invested in. Smaller investors find this sort of fund appealing because it achieves maximum diversification of risk. Realistically, they cannot do this for themselves because, with smaller amounts of money, the costs of doing so are too invidious to justify it. The disadvantage of this type of fund is that the investor pays two sets of annual management fees (see Asset Allocation, Collective Funds, Diversification, Front-End Loading, Managed Funds, Multi-Manager Funds, Unit Trust).

Futures

See Derivatives.

G

Gearing (US Leverage)

The Americans call this leverage. Leverage and gearing both mean the same thing: borrowings. The amount of gearing depends on how much money you've borrowed. Just as you might have a mortgage that represents 90 per cent of the cost of your house, in the same way a company can be 90 per cent geared. Before the bank blithely lends you a very large wodge of money to buy your house, it actually takes the precaution of looking at your cash flow to decide how much you can afford to borrow. It then takes a good look at what you're planning to buy to be sure that if, in a worst case scenario, you default on payment, the bank can sell the house (or whatever) to pay off the mortgage or loan. In a similar way, when a company is looking to borrow a large amount of cash, the bank will analyse its gearing ratio (amongst other things) to suss out how much debt the company's finances can cope with:

$$\frac{\text{Net Borrowings}}{\text{Shareholder's Funds}} \times 100 = \text{Gearing Ratio}\,(\%)$$

The bank also makes jolly sure that the company's cash flow covers its interest and debt repayments and ensures that repayments are not too lumpy, ie, not paid back all at once, but evenly spread. And it goes without saying that the prospects for that particular company as well as for its industry sector play an important part in the bank's decision whether to hand over the lolly or not. As an investor, be aware of the importance of gearing. For most companies, some gearing is desirable. However, whether high gearing is risky or not depends hugely on all sorts of factors, including the individual circumstances of a company, the industry it's operating in, and the competence of the management.

Gilt-Edged

Means really good quality. It is the term used to describe UK government bonds and other IOUs that are supposed to be default-proof. Let me stress that gilt-edged is meant to denote good quality, but there are occasional exceptions to this, like the Russian government's bond default in 1998. Note that this was the first time that Russia had EVER defaulted on any loan in the post-Czarist regime, so even though investors cheerfully regarded buying Russian bonds as a pretty safe bet, they were proved wrong (see AAA, Bonds, Credit Rating, Gilts).

Gilt/Equity Ratio

This is a usually pretty incomprehensible graph that measures the 'risk-free' returns offered by UK government bonds, also called gilts, against the dividend yield on shares (see Dividend Yield). It enables investors to determine whether shares are cheap or expensive in comparison with the 'risk-free' returns offered by gilts. Why do they bother with this? Well, history tells us that gilts have offered a return of between one-and-a half and three times the dividend yield of shares. But this is slightly misleading as it excludes the capital returns we get from holding shares over the long term. The rough guide is that (in theory at least) if this ratio drops below two, shares are likely to go up. However, if this number is two-and-a-half or three, shares could be set for a fall. Don't ask me why, but it is a ratio that will get a stockbroker's knickers in a twist if he feels he is on to something good.

Gilts

The general term used to describe government bonds, generally deemed to be effectively risk-free investments. Redeemable/dated, irredeemable/undated all refer to the lifespan of the bond (see Longs, Mediums and Shorts). They all share one characteristic though, and that is that they offer lenders interest on the loan in the form of twice-yearly paid coupons. The returns, in the form of interest payments, are also called 'yield' (see Bonds, Coupon, Gilt-Edged, Yield).

Global Depositary Receipts

See Depositary Receipts.

Gold

Gold is a commodity, just like pork bellies or soya beans. The only difference is that it's a lot harder to get at, necessitating digging it out of the ground. Pigs are easier to access, generally speaking. So while gold is merely a commodity, it does have scarcity value, and therefore people like to own it on the basis that it's a lot prettier to hang a bar of gold around your neck than a pig's trotter. In the past, investors have used gold as a hedge against inflation and some still do. Gold shares were staggeringly popular in the 1970s when the oil price shock sent inflation spiralling upwards. Since high inflation has fallen over the years, central banks have been steadily reducing their gold reserves. Now the spectre of deflation looms and the arguments for owning gold are less convincing. I wouldn't rule out stashing away the odd ingot here and there, but only as a very small percentage of my investment portfolio. As Gray Jolliffe puts it, 'The gold is nice. Frankincense and myrrh we've got plenty of!'

Golden Handcuffs

When the top brass of a company deems you to be such a valuable and indispensable member of the team that they cannot contemplate losing you, they show just how keen they are to hang on to you by securing you to your desk with a pair of golden handcuffs. The fact that the handcuffs are made of real gold shows how much they esteem you. The truth is even better. The bosses offer you large wodges of money to stay on board, kind of buying your loyalty. Naturally they're wily about it. They're not quite daft enough to give you all the money in one go (which is a great pity really). They offer you a starting wodge to whet your appetite, then they promise you more wodges in segments over a pretty long period of time, so you feel sufficiently incentivized to stay on.

Golden Handshake

You get this if you've been a valuable and esteemed member of the team, and the management of a company is gutted to see you go. Actually in reality, this is a glorified sacking. It's the pay-off you get, if your employment contract was negotiated well enough, when the bosses decide to terminate the contract earlier than planned. They then smile sadly, shake your hand and bid you adieu, or hold a wild boozy party to hail your departure, and slip you a wodge of money, bar of gold or something like it to show their appreciation of your 'inestimably valuable contribution to the company'.

Golden Hello

You've probably guessed by now that the lucky few who are lured away from existing employers (who on earth does this actually happen to?) are given a warm smile and a hello with bells on in the shape of lots of lovely lolly to tear themselves away from their already highly paid jobs and jump ship for even more pay, benefits, etc. Oh, to be so popular!

Golden Parachute

'Look out for number one!' is the common cry of incompetent bosses who've messed things up at their company and are now facing the unwelcome prospect of being booted off the board as a predator prowls round threatening to take it over. The incompetents, having already anticipated the disaster of their own demise, have by now made sure that they'll get paid lots of money in compensation for being unceremoniously sacked in the event of a takeover.

Goodwill

Why does the stock market ascribe a value to a company over and above the assets that it owns? Because the company's ability to generate profits from those assets also derives from intangible things like customer loyalty. A restaurant, for example, will have a regular clientele. When it is sold, the fact that it has existing customers makes the restaurant more valuable to the buyer than just the table and chairs. This added value is called goodwill and is listed under 'intangible assets' in a company's balance sheet. It's what a business builds up over the years by being reliable with its customers and damned good at what it does. It is difficult to place an absolute value on goodwill because it is intangible (see Accounts, Intangible Assets).

Government Bonds

See Gilts.

Grey Market

I'm not sure why this is called the grey market, as opposed to green or blue. It is when bold market-makers start to trade in shares, etc, ie, 'make a market' in them, when they are not yet officially listed on the stock market (see Market-Maker, Trader).

Gross Domestic Product – GDP

Measures the output of the economy. Domestic product is all the goods and services we produce minus net property income from overseas. Net property income from overseas is the income from assets owned by UK residents in other countries (foreign shares, for example) minus income from UK assets held by foreign residents. It doesn't really give us a terribly reliable idea of the health of the economy because the numbers used from different sources are not comparable.

Gross National Product – GNP

Measures the output of the economy. National product is all the goods and services we produce plus net property income from overseas (see Gross Domestic Product for explanation). This number doesn't really give us a terribly reliable idea of the health of the economy because the numbers used from different sources are not comparable.

Group of Ten

The bods who control the purse strings of the ten richest non-communist countries (finance ministers and top treasury officials if you really want their official titles) belong to a club called the Group of Ten. They get together as and when they feel it's necessary, usually to marshal financial support for one of its members that's hit a glitch. The ten are: Belgium, Canada, France, Germany, Great Britain, Italy, Japan, The Netherlands, Sweden and the United States.

Growth Funds

Funds that are invested in shares, which a fund manager expects to offer fast, good growth prospects in terms of earnings per share, dividend and capital growth of the shares (see Collective Funds, Distribution Funds, Growth Shares, Investment Trust, Income Funds, Managed Funds, Unit Trust).

Growth Shares

These are shares of companies listed on the Stock Exchange that are bought by investors anticipating that they will show good growth in profits. This in turn will lead to the shares going up, ie, capital appreciation of the shares. Because they are often very fast-growing businesses, they rarely offer much income by way of dividends as the company tends to plough profits back into itself in order to keep growing at the same rate. It's important to note that this type of share trades at very toppy (City slang for too high!)

valuations because investor expectations are so high. Consequently there is little room for manoeuvre. If the company fails to fulfil growth expectations, shareholders are liable to dump the shares. The reason is that an awful lot of good news is anticipated and included in the share price in advance. The City says, 'It is better to travel than to arrive.' Of course, good growth shares just keep on travelling but those that disappoint tend to arrive at their destination rather suddenly and brutally! (See Income Shares, Value Shares.)

Guaranteed Equity Bonds – GEB

Guarantees aren't always as enticing as they seem to be at first glance. Insurance companies and building societies offer guaranteed equity bonds, or GEBs. Basically they promise you the upside of investing in the stock market without the risk. You get stock market exposure, but your capital is safe because it will be returned to you at the end of the bond's life, together with any money made on the performance of the stock market. Sounds too good to be true? The disadvantages: you are locked in for a long time, so it's inflexible and you are also not guaranteed to get any return from the bond. Often, you won't benefit from the full extent of a rising stock market index, because the provider has to use some of that increase to cover its costs for offering you the capital protection in the first place. Oh, and it's non-marketable, so you cannot offload it on to someone else.

Guaranteed Growth Bonds – GGB

Similar to guaranteed income bonds (see Guaranteed Income Bonds below), only instead of paying out a regular fixed return, or income, over the life of the bond, you get it all in one hit as a lump sum at the end of the bond's life.

Guaranteed Income Bonds – GIB

These are bonds offered to investors by insurance companies that offer a set rate of income, also known as return or yield (see Yield).

A GIB is non-marketable, hence can't be flogged to anyone else, and inflexible because you are locked in for the length of the bond's life. However, the capital will be repaid at the end. GIBs look good when interest rates are falling, because you're locked into a higher return than the market, but they look less attractive when interest rates rise.

Guru

You are more likely to get fiscal enlightenment from financial gurus than the spiritual variety. A financial guru is someone whom everybody worships, believing him to be so awesomely clever, that he or she can predict what the stock market is going to do next. Financial gurus include Warren Buffett, George Soros and Peter Lynch. They have reached almost saint-like status, as people hang on to their every utterance in the hope that just listening to them will somehow miraculously improve their wealth. True, these guys are very smart and undoubtedly people whose opinions are to be respected. But a word of caution. Even the best of them makes mistakes. They, just like us, are fallible. The only difference is that, given the size of the funds they are managing, they can afford to lose the odd million here or there, whereas you and I can't! (See Financial Information.)

Health Insurance

Insurance that covers you in case you are sick. But there are different types of sickness. Short-term acute (wonderful euphemism) setbacks to your health, like those dodgy tonsils or a dicky appendix. Then there's the bolt from the blue, hideous accident (I'm touching wood that this should never happen to any of us), or there are long-term debilitating conditions. You can just see the actuary's eyes light up as he assesses the risk of this happening to individuals, depending on how risky their professional lives are. And yes, you guessed it, there's insurance for all, even bungee-jumping, parachuting, white-water rafting fearless types. The insurers have worked out quite skilfully, that for every one unfortunate person who makes a claim, there are millions of us who cheerfully trundle through life not claiming. So guess who wins? Even so, I reckon that health cover is jolly useful to have, especially for the ever-increasing ranks of the self-employed, who have no one offering super-deluxe corporate health care in the event that we should suffer a serious health setback, like an ingrown toenail. Anyway, here are the four types:

Accident and Sickness Cover

This is actually the most expensive type of protection because it promises to pay your bills and a substantial part of your income for short-term illnesses lasting no more than a year, with immediate effect from the onset of the health problem you suffer.

Critical Illness Cover

You pay regular monthly premiums with the promise of a large lump sum if you are unlucky enough to experience a sudden critical illness like a stroke, a heart attack or a brain tumour. It's useful to protect against unexpected serious illness and is affordable. A good one to have, methinks.

Permanent Health Insurance

Also called an income protection policy, this pays you a regular income that replaces about 60 per cent of your own income if you are unfortunate enough to be struck by an ongoing illness or disability, and it's tax-free! It's called PHI for short. It is a useful cover especially for the self-employed who cannot afford to get sick so easily. The only snag is that it is quite costly. Many of the policies are prohibitively expensive unless you agree to postpone the payout for at least three months from the start of your health troubles. The longer they delay payment, the more affordable this type of insurance gets, but you have to specify the non-payout period at the start of the policy. A good independent financial adviser should be able to shop around for you and get you a very competitive quote from a suitable health insurer (see Independent Financial Adviser).

Private Health Care Insurance

This enables you to see a specialist for your particular brand of hypochondria in double-quick time, instead of relying on the valiant, but ever more creaking National Health Service that just might let you pop your clogs before you get to see anyone about your life-threatening bout of housemaid's knee. It also pays your medical bills when you get sick. I reckon this type of insurance is almost indispensable.

Hedge Fund

You might assume that since hedging means using derivatives to protect your financial assets against risk, that hedge funds do the same. Boy, what a hideously wrong assumption that would be! The term 'hedge fund' encompasses a wide range of different types of fund management. A common theme with them is the use of derivatives. Some managers of hedge funds use derivatives to lower risk in the pursuit of steady returns. Others, bless their cotton socks, use derivatives aggressively to obtain leverage, ie, they take gigantic risks using futures and the like, which sometimes pay off. When they hit the jackpot, they make an obscene load of money. Unfortunately the reverse is also true. When the bets go wrong, they lose their shirts, along with the shirts of the unlucky investors that they've persuaded to participate in the fund. What's crucial is to understand which type you are buying into, if indeed you decide to go for this type of fund at all. It's a very specialized area, which needs exceptionally good expert advice so investors are under no illusions about what they are getting into (see Derivatives, Fund Management).

Hedging

Hedging your bets, in investment terms, is supposed to mean making sure that you cover your back with insurance should anything go wrong. It offers protection against downside risk. In share markets, often the best way to do this is to use options, the traditional or traded variety (see Derivatives – Options). But some options are so risky that they need to be hedged themselves, or you can get unstuck with them.

High-Yield Shares

There is usually a good reason why a company's shares offer a better return than the market. There is often, though not always, a catch. It could be that the business has stopped growing. Or the company is in deep debt, and enticing suckers to part with their cash is difficult, so they are forced to offer a better return (in the form of dividends) than the market's average share return. So, as with any other investment, MORE RETURN MEANS MORE RISK! There are high-yielding companies that are reasonably safe, but investors have to tread carefully and assess in their own minds what the real risks are. If in doubt, don't buy! (See Income Shares, Risk, Risk/Reward Ratio, Yield.)

HM Revenue & Customs

Shock horror! The Inland Revenue has merged with HM Customs & Excise to make a new super-duper overarching tax collector.

Now that the two organizations have joined forces, it is a comfort to know that this has all been done solely in the name of making the dreaded collection of tax and all other tax-related matters simpler and easier to deal with for us mere mortals! If you want to visit its new website and spend hours poring over vital new ways of receiving tax bills and even tax credits, see www.hmrc.gov.uk.

Home Income Plan

It's a way for more mature people, 65-plus, to get an income from assets they own, like property, and thus release tied-up capital. Say you own a mortgage-free home. You could take out a mortgage on it that would buy you an annuity (see Pension – Annuity). Part of the money you get will be tax-free (the capital); the remainder is subject to income tax. This is a pretty complicated area, which I reckon needs specialist advice from a good independent financial adviser (see Equity Release, Independent Financial Adviser).

Hyperinflation

When the government prints lots of money to get itself out of trouble, it has the effect of making money worth less; this is inflation. Prices, as well as the value of assets such as property, shares and art tend to go up in these circumstances. Sometimes inflation spirals out of control. It is when a government prints too much money too quickly and continues to do so over a long period of time. The corollary to this is that prices go up very fast and the value of money goes down equally fast. When inflation exceeds 20 per cent per annum, it is classed as hyperinflation. In a final resort, when trying to control the level of the country's currency proves useless, the government will allow its currency to devalue. This, of course, is also inflationary, so don't get confused by the 'de' in devaluation. Everyone agrees that too much inflation is a bad thing and thankfully that threat seems to have receded in the United Kingdom, Europe and the United States. Now the big worry is deflation, ie, prices and asset values falling, which include property prices, art and the stock market. This isn't good news either. In this instance investors cry 'Cash is king!' (See Deflation, Devaluation, Disinflation, Inflation.)

Illiquid

The opposite to liquid, obviously! This is the posh way of describing investments that are not very easy to buy and sell. Or more bluntly, a pig to try to get in and out of. In a stock market sense it tends to refer to shares in smaller companies that are not very actively traded. The natural corollary to illiquid shares (or any other illiquid investment for that matter) is that they are a whole lot more volatile (see Beta, Liquid, Thin Market, Volatility).

Income

Income is money received by us from various sources and which we tend to live off. One form of it is money earned through our own efforts, in terms of a salary or wage. The other main source is money generated by things we possess. Examples are shares paying dividends, bonds that pay interest, or cash earning interest on deposit in the building society. The Inland Revenue likes to call this unearned income. All the above are liable to income tax (see Tax – Income Tax). In Jane Austen's time, when people were said to be on '£10,000 a year' it meant that they had an income of £10,000 a year (this was a hell of a lot those days. Come hither Mr Darcy!), which was being generated from their capital and investments (see Capital).

Income Funds

These are investment funds that provide an attractive yield or return to investors. Because the people who buy into these funds seek income in the form of high returns, the prospect for underlying capital growth in the shares is sometimes sacrificed. The more mature investor might well want income to supplement a pension. Younger investors are often willing to forgo short-term income with a view to seeing their shares or investments rise in value over the long term (see Collective Funds, Distribution Funds, Growth Funds, Income Shares, Managed Funds, Unit Trust, Yield).

Income Shares

Shares that give you an income! They offer you a stream of money in the shape of dividend payouts (otherwise known as yield). Generally when we buy income shares, we don't expect them to be really super-stud performers and go to the moon. More often than not, they are big businesses that operate in a mature market, and show sluggish growth, but generate very good cash flows and pay good, regular dividends. These types of shares tend to suit people who don't want to take enormous amounts of risk but do want the regular income that they can get from a reasonably solid safe company. Similar, but more high risk, are high-yielding shares (see High-Yield Shares).

Income Yield

When a borrower raises money by issuing bonds, it usually pays the lender interest, the amount of which is based on the price paid for the bonds in the market. This interest, or return, is also known as the income yield. Example: suppose a company issues a £100 bond that offers the lender 5 per cent per annum over its lifetime. The income yield at that point is 5 per cent. So far, so good. But what happens if the price of the £100 bond, which is being traded freely on the bond market, falls to £50? The bond's income yield will automatically rise to 10 per cent because of the mathematical rules of the bond market – when the underlying price of a bond falls, its return goes up, and vice versa (see Bonds, Redemption Yield, Yield).

Independent Financial Adviser – IFA

In an ideal world, you meet the perfect independent financial adviser who will put you into the best pension plan, the best life insurance policy, the best mortgage, the best ISAs and unit trusts, etc. Completely impartial, he will not be swayed by the temptation of big fat commissions from insurers, pension providers and mortgage lenders. At least, that is the theory. Welcome to the real world. With several thousand IFAs to choose from, finding the right one for you could be a nightmare. These people can be useful because they take so much of the legwork out of the dreary task of getting yourself a mortgage, etc. They shop around and know about all the best deals of the moment.

First stop, ask friends if they know a good IFA. Failing that, check out the website: www.unbiased.co.uk. This will give you a lot of information about IFAs and guide you to a number of them listed in your area.

When you first meet an IFA, you want reassurance from him that he is completely independent and will give you best advice. Test his knowledge. And if you don't like or trust the person, don't even think about going any further. Meet several IFAs until you find one you do trust and you feel will act in your best interests over the long term. The watchword here is caution. Because pensions and life insurance, etc are all long-term commitments, do not rush decisions. Be like a reluctant virginal bride and take your time.

Be aware that an IFA must give you a menu outlining both his fee and commission-charging options and that he is obliged to offer you this 'fees' option. Feel free to grill him on which method of payment would be best for you. Don't hold back. This is your money and you have to take charge. It's no good whinging ten years after the event and wishing you hadn't been so compliant with the IFA who roped you into the wrong mortgage or pension.

Far better to be more assertive and ask the right questions now. This is where you can really go to town and be as pedantic and nit-picking as you like! Ask things like the following:

- Are you authorized to give investment advice?
- Are you truly independent and not tied to any particular company?
- How are you paid for giving me your wonderful, impartial advice?
- How much is it going to cost me?
- How much are you being paid for selling me this product?
- Why have you chosen this product over that?
- Do other similar products pay you less commission?
- If so, what's wrong with the cheaper ones?
- Is the commission I'm paying you front end-loaded (ie, paid to the adviser all upfront as soon as he or she has shifted, sorry, sold the product!) or do you get paid evenly over a period of years? (Obviously the latter is preferable for you.)
- How will the commission charges affect the performance of my investment?
- Since I'm putting squillions of my hard-earned cash into your highly recommended 'Crumbling Edifice' Fund, how about refunding some of the commission to me?
- Can I pay in fees, ie, per hour, rather than in commission? If so, will your advice work out cheaper, dearer or about the same?
- How do you actually research your investment recommenda-tions? (This is VERY important to you, dear reader, as it's one way of finding out who knows their onions from those who don't!)
- What happens if I change my mind a year or two down the tracks? Will I be charged any penalties and how much money will I get back?
- Will this product tie me in, or can I change my mind and walk away without penalties at any stage? And so on.

A lot of these questions are common sense, but don't be a shrinking violet. You have every right to know how your money will be spent. Whether you pay fees only or accept commission-based advice depends on what you'd be happiest with. Be sure to make an informed choice and DO make comparisons with what other advisers are offering.

If you agree to pay 'fees-only' to an adviser, and not commission, the good news is that any commission he would have earned goes to you. It does no harm to make sure that you are actually getting this money. Most advisers working on this basis will be only too anxious to show you that they have rebated you the commission, so you can have peace of mind that they're not trying to pull a fast one (see Commission, Financial Adviser, Tied Financial Adviser).

Alarm bells should ring if someone offers you very attractive returns on your money without risk. If the banks and building societies, shares and bonds are offering returns of, say, 5 per cent per annum, then an investment that will double your money, risk-free, in 12 months is a pretty obvious no-no. Ask yourself why someone is offering you such superior returns and remember the risk/reward ratio (see Risk/Reward Ratio).

If you've been unlucky enough to have been mis-sold a product, step one is to go back to the adviser and seek compensation; if you are unhappy with their response you can then go to the Financial Ombudsman Service and enlist its help; its website is: www.fos.org.uk. If the adviser has gone bust, then your last resort is to seek redress from the Financial Services Compensation Scheme, but only if the company you dealt with was authorized (see Financial Services Authority). If you think you might have a case, contact them at: www.fscs.org.uk.

Index

A stock market index measures the general financial health of the market. It also allows you to see whether it is going up or down. You can compare one stock market with another and also check out whether the shares you own are doing better or worse than the market as a whole (see Outperform, Underperform).

Broadly speaking, an index is made up by calculating the value of all the companies it follows and doing some mathematical wizardry, which you don't need to worry your head about to make the index meaningful over a long period of time. In the United Kingdom, the *Financial Times* publishes a plethora of indices that it has constructed and assiduously follows. The most widely used ones are the following:

The FTSE 100, also known as Footsie, follows the fortunes of the top 100 UK companies. The FTSE 250 does the same for the 250 next biggest companies after the Footsie. After that comes the FTSE 350 and so on.

Every stock market in the world has its own main index, like our FTSE 100, which is followed by investors. In particular, they all obsessively follow the American Dow Jones Industrial Average (DJIA), because the US stock market is the largest in the whole world, and its behaviour has an impact on other stock markets (see Dow Jones 500, Dow Jones Industrial Average, Footsie, Tracker Funds).

Index-Linked

Also known as indexation: any 'index-linked' investment, price, salary, etc, is linked to the rate of inflation. Just because an investment is 'index-linked' doesn't mean that it is automatically worth buying, but at least you have the comfort of knowing that the returns you get will be linked to the Retail Price Index, which is the United Kingdom's measure of inflation (see Inflation, National Savings Certificates, Retail Price Index).

Index-Linked Gilts

These are the main type of tradable index-linked investments. They are UK government bonds (see Gilts) that, as they pay you returns over the years, adjust for any inflation in the financial system. So if during the lifetime of a bond, inflation caused prices to double (hopefully an unlikely scenario), you'd get twice the value of the bond when the government was due to pay the loan off.

Individual Savings Account – ISA

Well, if you've got a degree in quantum physics, you may well be able to work out just how an ISA works. For the rest of us mere mortals, it's a bit of a struggle. The government hasn't exactly bent over backwards to make these really useful things user-friendly for us.

There are two types of ISA, a mini and a maxi. If you go for a mini (or minis), you CANNOT go for a maxi in the same year. The minis have to be one or both of £3000 in cash, or £4000 in 'stocks and shares'. The maxi lets you put £7000 into shares only. Any of these ISAs can include insurance products.

The principle behind an ISA is that it acts like a container. Whatever you decide to pop into the ISA container, H M Revenue & Customs can't get at. Hurray! So if, a few years down the track, you choose to sell or withdraw whatever was in it, you won't have to pay tax on the proceeds, profits or income you received from it. To enjoy this tax break, your money has to stay in this container. The good news is that even if you change your mind about the nature of the investment, you can swap it within the ISA and still protect the tax-free element. Important to note is that cash investments can only be swapped for other cash investments and 'stocks and shares' investments can only be swapped for, yes you guessed it, 'stocks and shares' investments. You can't swap 'stocks and shares' into cash.

Inflation

Sir Stafford Cripps, the Labour Chancellor in office just after World War II, put it very succinctly when he described inflation as 'too much money chasing too few goods'. When the government prints lots of money to stop the economy from nose-diving into recession, this creates inflation. Prices and wages rise. The stock market booms and so does the property market. Why? Because, generally speaking, there are only a fixed number of shares and houses on offer. Lots of extra money in the financial system just pushes prices up further. There is much talk about the death of inflation, but when have you known prices to stay the same or to go down over a really long period of time? (See Deflation, Disinflation, Hyperinflation.)

Inside Information

Anyone who has access to this type of information has a better than even chance of actually making money on the stock market. This is the low-down, the really juicy info that will immediately affect the price of a share the minute it's let out into the public domain. Of course the regulatory bods out there have put paid to the pleasure of 'insiders' (people with access to this privileged information) being able to use inside or 'price-sensitive' information to their advantage. In the good old days everybody did it and made money for themselves and their investors. Now that insider trading is illegal, huge swarms of compliance officers and regulatory bureaucrats zealously scour the City in search of the wrongdoer who might be making illicit gains (see Chinese Walls, Compliance, Financial Services Authority, Insider Dealing).

Insider Dealing

Lots of people in the City are privy to inside or 'price-sensitive' information. However, contrary to popular belief that they're all at it like rabbits (insider dealing that is!) most people don't actually take advantage of it. The simple reason is that it's totally illegal to do so and it's not worth jeopardizing lucrative career prospects for a paltry few thousand quid's illicit profit. However, there are some chancers in life, and they just get a real thrill out of trying to get the better of the authorities, so I rather suspect it does go on. To prevent this nefarious activity, the trusty compliance officer (see Compliance) comes galloping along and tries to rescue potential wrongdoers from their own greed. He either gets to them before they use the inside information or institutes disciplinary proceedings after the dastardly act. In reality, the perpetrator is fired from his job, fined and barred from working in the City. He might even do a spot of porridge!

Institutional Investors

These are the big cheeses in the world of stock market investment, and the ones that all the City stockbroking firms suck up to the most. They control billions of pounds in the shape of pension funds', life assurance companies' or individuals' money in collective funds such as unit trusts or investment trusts, which are managed by fund managers. The 500 shares you and I own in British Telecom are infinitesimally small in comparison to the shares, bonds and other assets, such as property, that these institutional investors invest in. They are without doubt the movers and shakers of international stock markets (see Collective Funds, Managed Funds, Investment Trust, Unit Trust).

Intangible Assets

Things belonging to a business that are invisible. You cannot touch, see or feel them, but they are worth money nonetheless. Obvious examples are things like patents. A business might own the exclusive patent to make a hideously complicated Soup-o-Miser. The patent is patently worth money, and is shown in a company's balance sheet as an asset, albeit an intangible one. The main types of intangible asset are brand names, copyrights, trademarks and goodwill (see Goodwill, Tangible Assets).

Interest

There's no such thing as a free lunch. (Hey, that's a great title for a book!) If you borrow money from someone, whether it's a mortgage lender or a credit card company, they will be very interested to get their money back, with interest. You have to pay it to them for the privilege of temporarily getting your hands on their loot. Conversely, if you put money on deposit in a building society or buy National Savings Certificates (amongst other possibilities) they are so grateful to get their mitts on your cash that they confer on you the honour of paying you interest. Whichever way around, the principle is the same. There are a huge number of banks and building societies out there where you can deposit your cash. All offer a very wide range of returns or interest on your money.

A very good way to find out who is offering the most favourable rates is to consult the Moneyfacts website: www.moneyfacts.co.uk. Another good way to check rates is in the personal finance sections of the national newspapers, like *Telegraph Money* or *Financial Mail on Sunday*, for example (see AER – Annual Equivalent Rate, APR – Annual Percentage Rate, EAR – Equivalent Annual Rate).

Interest Cover

Companies frequently borrow money. Why? Oh, all the usual reasons. They want to expand their operations, make the business bigger, improve their day-to-day cash flow. When those industrious analysts wade through all the numbers in a company's accounts, trying to suss what state its finances are in, they love to check out the interest cover. It's a really easy mathematical calculation:

$$\frac{\text{Profit Before Interest and Tax}}{\text{Interest Payable}} = \text{Interest Cover}$$

The City people are a cautious lot; they like the reassurance of knowing that, if interest rates were to rise suddenly, a business can still comfortably pay its interest bill to whomever it owes money. The higher this number, the more analysts and future potential lenders will rest easy and relax (see Asset Cover, Dividend Cover).

Interest Rate

Governments or central banks set a country's national interest rate. The level they fix it at affects how much the banks and building societies charge for borrowing money and conversely, what they will pay for cash deposited with them. In the United Kingdom, the government has handed the responsibility of interest rate setting to the Bank of England.

Interest rates are used to try to control the economy's growth. If it looks as though growth is steaming ahead too fast, the government or central bank will raise rates to dampen down the economy and prevent it overheating. If the government has gone too far, ie, raised rates too high, it stalls the economy too much and things grind to a halt rather suddenly: this is recession. So then the government panics and brings interest rates down again. It's rather clumsy, but probably one of the more effective methods of trying to control the vagaries of a free market economy (see Bank of England, Base Rate, Boom/Bust, Central Bank).

International Monetary Fund

Along with the World Bank, this is also a super-large monetary fund that acts as a buffer to prevent countries that look in danger of going belly up from doing so. How does it do this? By lending them money, usually with strict performance and reform criteria, while they pull themselves up out of their short-term difficulties.

In the Money

'We're in the money!' is not an altogether inaccurate description of this one. Back to the world of options, where the thrill of making money is somewhat akin to a day at Newmarket racecourse. When you buy a call or put option (see Derivatives – Options), you pay a small sum of money to secure the right to buy or sell shares at a fixed price at some point in the future. If, in the meantime, the shares in which you own the option are trading at a higher price than the price you originally fixed it at, then the option is 'in the money'. It means that if, for instance, you were to exercise your right to buy those shares at this predetermined option price, you would instantly make a profit if you chose to sell them in the market immediately afterwards. The exact converse is true when your options are 'out of the money' (see At the Money, Out of the Money).

Investment

The general, loose term we use to describe the action of putting, ie, investing, our hard-earned cash into things that we have carefully researched and hope will grow in value over a period of time. It is not punting on the options market, or buying shares, bonds or whatever today, with a view to making a quick killing tomorrow. That's trading territory and falls under the high-risk tag of speculation, not investment (see Long-Term Investment, Short-Term Investment, Trader).

Investment Bank

Also called merchant banks or, less commonly, issuing houses, these banks are not run-of-the-mill retail banks that cater to the likes of you and me. They offer a range of specialist services to companies or institutional investors. The corporate broking department offers companies advice and help on how to raise money via the Stock Exchange. Advice is given on many levels, including whether it is reckoned appropriate for companies to gain a Stock Exchange quotation at their particular stage in development. If a company does elect to issue its shares through a particular investment bank, it (the bank) will offer those shares to its institutional clients. Small investors like you and I rarely get the benefit of a 'hot' juicy new issue (see New Issue). However, we benefit indirectly, because those hot issues end up in our pension funds, life assurance funds, etc.

The M&A department (short for Mergers & Acquisitions) within an investment bank is usually the most lucrative part of its business. The guys who populate this world are corporate financiers. They spend their time advising companies what bits of their businesses they should be getting rid of, as well as types of business to be on the lookout for when they are expanding. When a bid or acquisition is successful, the fees can be stratospheric. Of course, you have to remember that for every successful deal, there are many that fail (see Corporate Finance, Due Diligence, Mergers & Acquisitions).

Investment Management Association – IMA

This is a trade body that represents all the professional fund management groups, which in turn are its members. If you're considering buying unit trusts with your money (see Unit Trust), there are an awful lot of them to choose from. With over 1,500 on offer, it would be astonishing if you weren't confused. The IMA has some useful fact sheets and guides that will give you a clearer idea of what's what. The next thing you'll want to know is how these unit trusts stack up against each other. There are two sources you can consult if you've decided to put your money into pooled investments like this: monthly magazine, *Money Management*, which lists the unit trust pop charts, ie, the best and worst, and Micropal, which provides detailed fund performance statistics. Useful websites to visit are: www.investmentuk.org and www.micropal.com.

Investment Trust

The name is a bit confusing, because this is not a trust. An investment trust (IT) is actually a company whose shares are freely traded on the stock market in the same way as BP, Sainsbury's or Vodafone shares. An IT does pretty much everything a company can, such as borrow money to buy assets, and issue long-term bonds and debentures. It only has a fixed amount of shares in issue, which makes it a closed-end fund (see Closed-End Funds, Open-End Funds).

A unit trust, by contrast, has constant cash inflows and outflows as investors pour money into it or make redemptions, ie, withdraw their money out of it. You just put your money into a unit trust and you become the proud owner of units in it. Investing in an IT means you are buying shares in a company that owns shares in other companies. A key factor that makes an IT attractive or unattractive is the value of its assets, or net asset value per share in City-speak (see Net Asset Value per Share). Many ITs trade at discounts to their net asset values, so they can be interesting investments. However, just because an IT is looking 'cheap' doesn't automatically mean that it is sexy and must be bought at once. As ITs can sometimes borrow very heavily, this type of investment is potentially much higher risk than a unit trust, which is not allowed to do so (see Association of Investment Trust Companies).

Invisibles

This means things people pay for that you cannot see. Examples are services such as banking, shipping and tourism, which provide a country with revenue. As these are intangible services, ie, you cannot touch or feel them, they've been given the inspired title of invisibles! Other invisibles are intellectual property; examples are royalties from television rights or movies. The more invisibles a country exports, the more money (revenue) it gets paid into its current account.

Issue

Not a nasty reaction to the excessive pollen and pollution in the air. It is the general word that means the sale of shares or bonds to the investment community, which includes fund management groups, pension funds and life assurance companies, as well as private individuals like you and me (see Investment Bank, New Issue).

J

J Curve

Economic gobbledygook for things getting worse before they get better, following an event like the lowering of interest rates. It's a funny J-shaped squiggle on a chart. The reason why this economic phrase has its name is because the bottom of the letter 'J' dips down and then goes up!

Jobbers

In the good old days, long before deregulation, the City was a much smaller pond than it is now. It was a cosy little club and there were clearly defined lines between different functions. The jobber was a principal, ie, he risked his own capital buying and selling shares. Stockbrokers would come up to him and ask, 'What's your price in Bloggins plc?' and the jobber would make and give a price. How would he know what price to make? you ask. Sheer mathematical genius? Actually, no. He would be tuned in to the supply and demand for a particular share, and would adjust his prices accordingly. It was all very civilized (well, most of the time) and business transacted took place on the Stock Exchange trading floor. Things changed dramatically with the advent of the deregulation of the UK stock market (Big Bang) in 1986. Fixed commissions were abolished and the City opened its doors wide open to anyone who had enough capital to set up a brokerage firm. Today, all the jobbers have been absorbed into large, conglomerate-style banks that are multifunctional – they are stockbrokers, jobbers, corporate financiers, even bond issuers all rolled into one. You name it; these large corporate monoliths do it. Jobbers are now known as market-makers (see Chinese Walls, Dual Capacity, Market-Maker, Single Capacity).

Jobbing Backwards

Something we all do, but shouldn't. It's when we say things like 'If only I had bought shares in Microsoft ten years ago I'd be a multimillionaire by now' or 'If only I had known that Groggle plc shares were a complete dog, I would never have bought them'. Jobbing backwards is when we use the benefit of hindsight to make ourselves completely miserable as we contemplate things we should or shouldn't have done! However, I concede that it is useful to analyse one's investment cock-ups, if only to ensure that they won't happen again. And reading this book from cover to cover will help you down that hallowed path! But once you've dissected where and why and how things went horribly wrong, move on, and don't allow the bitter taste of regret to affect your future investment judgement calls and decisions. If I had a tenner for every 'If only!' I've uttered in my short little life I'd be ridiculously rich by now!

Junk Bonds

Like junk food, these are bonds that make you feel momentarily good but can have nasty side-effects afterwards. As the name implies, they are not the crème de la crème on offer to investors in the bond world. More like curdled crème. Junk bonds should carry a high-risk health warning. In order to compensate investors for this higher risk, the borrowers who issue them (companies that are on a shaky financial footing) pay a higher rate of interest than the more solid, safe ones. But buyer beware (*caveat emptor* for all you posh Latin speakers). The sexier it looks the riskier it usually is. Me, I do not have the bottle to put my money in this type of investment. Other more swashbuckling types who like to take big bets may find these attractive. More seriously, these bonds have poor credit ratings (see AAA, Bonds, Credit Rating, Mezzanine Finance).

Kondratieff Cycle

Nikolai Kondratieff thought up the Kondratieff Cycle long before Sir Clive Sinclair invented the electric version. He was a pretty clever Russian who measured the big up and down undulations of the world economy. He basically observed that it has a tendency to make big up and down swings every 50 to 60 years or so. The Great Depression in the 1930s was the last major downward leg. Obviously, in between these super-cycles pinpointed by Kondratieff, he identified lots of little mini-cycles, up and down blips of global economic activity. If his thesis were correct, it would imply that we're due for a serious downswing sometime soon. The only problem is that history doesn't necessarily act as an accurate guide to the future. For example, it is possible that the time span of these super-cycles has lengthened. Which would mean a major economic glitch might be several years away. In any case, there seems little wisdom in panicking unduly yet. Incidentally, Kondratieff was awarded a special prize for his intellectual prowess. An extended stay at Stalin's luxurious Siberian salt mines!

L

Lagging Indicator

Economic-speak. It describes economic indicators whose numbers are published after the event. An example: inflation figures for April don't show up in government statistics until June, so it is a lagging indicator (see Leading Indicator).

Leading Indicator

Anything that seeks to project forward into the future is a leading indicator; hence the stock market is one. Why? Because if it starts to drop heavily, it could be warning us of worse economic times to come, such as a recession.

As well as doing a spot of crystal ball gazing, City economists zealously focus on specific lagging government statistics in order to try and predict the future. So lagging indicators can also be leading ones! These statistics are usually issued monthly and include stuff like manufacturing output, the retail price index (see Retail Price Index – RPI), producer price index and many others that you really do not need to worry about just now. The month-by-month numbers mean nothing in themselves. The main thing to note is that the City whiz-kids are looking for a trend that will give them valuable clues about the future direction of the country's economy. Every so often they throw a complete wobbly about, for example, a higher than expected RPI number – this is an indicator of inflation. They run around like headless chickens in horror and panic, and the stock market takes a dive. The funny thing is that for ages no one pays attention to these numbers. Then out of the blue, they take on an earth-shattering significance and have a major, albeit short-term, influence on the market.

Life Insurance

While I, as a single person, naturally debate the usefulness of a form of insurance that will only pay out when I am dead, there are millions of others who disagree and see it as a jolly useful thing, especially when the assured has a family to support. There are some that might wish to leave a handsome legacy to their pet duck or iguana, and who am I to cast a downer on such care and concern? Here are some of the different kinds of life insurance:

1. The cheapest and most straightforward type of life insurance is called 'term assurance'. It assures a payout of a lump sum of money if you are unlucky enough to drop off the perch within a pre-agreed period (also called the 'term'). However, it pays nothing if you have the temerity to survive that designated period. It is a very useful type of cover to protect your loved ones from being left horribly in the lurch if a bolt from the blue zaps you out of existence. It will assure things like the mortgage and school fees being paid, and prevent those left behind from experiencing dire penury. My instinct is that it's usually best to take out more cover than you think you actually need.

2. Another type of life insurance covers you whilst you are alive. The most common variety is 'whole of your life insurance' and it is designed to pay out to your beneficiaries. There are about 500 policies to choose from and this tends to be more expensive as the policies have to pay out, regardless.

3. Then there is an endowment, ie, a life insurance policy that invests the premium money in funds. This life assurance policy pays out or 'matures' on a pre-agreed date, regardless of whether the policyholder dies or not. This is an altogether trickier proposition and one that needs careful thought (see Endowment).

Limited Liability

You'll be thrilled to know that if you own shares in a limited
liability company that goes belly up, you only lose the money you
originally invested in the first place. Unlimited liability is the
converse, and is really bad news. This is definitely NOT something
you want to be a part of, because it means that if you are an
investor in a company that goes bust, you're liable for ALL its
losses and debts.

Limit Order

See At Limit.

Liquid Assets

Assets that you or a business possess that are closest to cash.

Liquidation

Sounds nasty, and guess what, it is! This is the rather squelchy
word used to describe a business that has been forced to close, ie,
gone bust. Official liquidators, who are usually accountants looking nothing like Arnold Schwarzenegger, are appointed to the
business that's writhing in its death throes to pick through the
bones of what they can sell off and what they have to write off as
unsaleable. They're doing this unpalatable job to repay the people
to whom the liquidated company owes money, ie, its creditors.
These folks are repaid according to strict rules. For a list of the
order in which shareholders of bankrupt companies get paid out,
look under Shares (see Bankrupt, Receiver).

Liquid/Liquidity

It describes the ease with which you can get in and out of shares
or indeed other investments. Therefore easily tradable things are

known as liquid and things that are a real bugger to buy and sell
are illiquid (see Illiquid).

Listing

When a company is brought to the stock market, it is 'listed' on the
Stock Exchange. Another phrase meaning the same thing is 'stock
market quotation' or 'quote'.

Loan Stock

See Corporate Bonds.

Local Authority Bonds

Local authorities borrow money, just like the rest of us. The only
difference is that they borrow tons more than we do. In return for
getting their mitts temporarily on our cash, they give us a bit of
paper called a bond promising to pay the loan back. In the meantime they pay interest on the money we've lent them, decent bunch
that they are. The bits of paper are officially called local authority
bonds or local authority stock. They have a lifespan of up to ten
years. The only snag with these type of bonds is that although they
behave just like other bonds, there is a very important distinction.
You can't flog them on to anyone else. They are not, repeat, not
tradable on the stock market. This little fact renders them pretty
inflexible. These type of bonds are really only useful for people
who are happy to tie up their money for a long time and only
expect a regular fixed income for themselves. They're not suitable
for those who might need sudden access to their cash in the near
term. (See Yearling Bonds.)

London Stock Exchange

See Stock Exchange.

Long

When a City type asks you if you are 'long' of something, do not feel embarrassed. It's nothing personal. He is just making a friendly enquiry as to whether you are the proud owner of a particular share. This also applies to certain assets they (usually no longer) want. One example might be, 'I'm long of an X-reg Porsche, great nick, CD player, Trafficmaster, hands-free mobile. Know anyone who's short?' Short naturally referring to the as yet unlucky individual who is not the proud owner of said Porsche (see Short, Square).

Longs

Also known as long-dated gilts, these are UK government bonds that have a lifespan of more than 15 years (see Gilts, Mediums, Shorts).

Long-Term Investment

This is all very subjective. To a trader, long term could mean a few minutes. To me, it means five to ten years. Sometimes when you've been stuffed into a share that's been steadily dropping in value since you bought it, it becomes a long-term investment, ie, one you can't afford to sell. The marketing blurb for funds always stresses the virtues of long-term investing, meaning at least five years. Yet fund managers are judged on their performance every three months. This short-termism is rampant in the City. So it's no surprise that when a company delivers one set of bad results, the big players drop it like a hot brick and switch their attention elsewhere. The problem is that once the institutions have dumped the shares, it's usually too late for you or me to sell our measly little holding in the same company. Bit like locking the stable door after the horse has bolted (see Short-Term Investment, Trader).

Managed Funds

Also called investment funds. Hopefully by now you're wised up to the fact that a fund contains the amalgamated money of lots of individuals. Managed funds are looked after by professionals called fund managers, who've been trained in the art of managing money so that it brings superior returns to the overall market (at least that's the theory). Being 'actively managed' they are the opposite of tracker funds. The money is spread over a widely diversified spectrum of investments, which includes shares, bonds, property and cash, hence reducing risk.

The other big advantage of these funds is that because such enormous sums of money are under management, they have huge economies of scale and can buy and sell shares at a tiny fraction of the costs to us as individuals (see Active Management, Diversification, Investment Management Association, Investment Trust, Tracker Funds, Unit Trust).

Management

Generally, the term applies to the bods who actually run a company, manage the employees and make earth-shattering decisions about where it is heading in terms of strategy and future direction. All directors are part of management, but not all of the management are directors. All sorts of fancy titles abound, such as chairperson and chief executive, managing director, executive director, director, etc. The proud bearer of a title is usually in charge of a specific area of the business. The exception is in the City, where directorships are doled out like candy to placate very successful salespeople who want to be in charge, but can't be because someone else is. This has given City firms, stockbrokers and the like, the celebrated reputation of having more chiefs than Indians (see Board of Directors).

Management Buy Out – MBO

When the directors or managers of a business buy up all or part of the company they are running. Often this happens because a large company wants to get rid of a part of its business and the directors of that division say, 'Hey, we'll buy it and run it ourselves!' It doesn't necessarily mean that the part is no good; it just might not fit in with the overall strategy of the bigger company any more (see Buy In Management Buy Out – BIMBO).

Margin

Means several things: see Spread. Margin also means the minimum collateral required to be put up by investors who are brave enough to dabble in options and futures. A third meaning is the amount of profit made by a company making widgets – this is the profit margin. Fourth and finally: margin is the percentage over and above the cost of money – ie, London Interbank Offered Rate or the base rate – charged to a borrower by a lender (see Floating Rate Note).

Margin Call

You only need to know this in theory because you are sensible and you're not going to put up margin to fool around with futures, are you? The reason is that if things go wrong, and your trade goes against you, the broker, who already has a small amount of your money, will come banging on your door and ask for more (ie, he'll 'call' for more 'margin'). Why? Because he wants to be sure that you're going to cough up for your futures contract. He doesn't really sympathize too much with the fact that you're already losing money big-time. He just wants concrete reassurance (in the form of cash) that you can cover your losses. The very thought of how much you can lose on this form of gambling gives me the heebie-jeebies (see Derivatives – Futures).

Margin Trading

This is borrowing money to invest in the stock market. In my books this is a complete no-no, the same as 'margin call'. While you make more profits on your investment than the cost of borrowing the money you are okay; however, if you make losses, it could be a bottomless pit. Margin trading can get you into deep trouble and you may end up reading my definition of Bankrupt.

Marketable Securities

Marketable securities are things you can enthusiastically buy and then flog in the stock market, etc when you've changed your mind and decided that owning Widgets plc shares or bonds was a hideous mistake. It goes without saying that you can't do this with non-marketable ones (see Non-Marketable Securities).

Market Capitalization

Multiply the number of shares in a company by its current share price and you arrive at its market capitalization. This is its total stock market value. Obviously this changes day to day as the share price fluctuates.

Market Influences

These are intangible things that affect investment markets and prices. Other grand-sounding names are market psychology and market sentiment. But surely, you say, it's just supply and demand that affects prices? You are absolutely right. But there are also other factors that affect the supply and demand for different shares and bonds, etc. Some of them make sense; others are more difficult to fathom. There are company-specific factors, such as a new product that's about to burst on to the shelves and make the company a fortune, or a new boss who's a red-hot manager and expected to turn an ailing business around. Then there are things that are general to the market, otherwise known as market sentiment, such as the outlook for interest rates or economic growth. Don't forget the constant rumours that fly around the dealing rooms of the City. Of course, the tricky bit is establishing if they are true or false!

Gauging whether it is the right time to invest is very difficult. There is always a good reason not to. At any time there could be an unexpected financial shock that severely shakes confidence and causes stock markets to fall out of bed. The trick is to remain unfazed by these things. If you've got the right shares and investments, then short-term financial nasties won't really make a dent in their value over the long term. And as for market timing, well, there aren't too many people who get it spot on. I've given up trying to predict the optimum moment to buy a share or a fund and come to the conclusion that if an investment looks sound and solid, with good long-term growth prospects, it is best to bite the bullet and buy. What about market psychology? If you follow the market closely enough, you'll start to see patterns repeated; when the euphoria and buoyancy of the market is overdone, or the doom and gloom has bottomed (see Financial Manias).

All the above offer valuable clues to the state of the stock market at any given time. Ultimately, the only thing that really matters is whether the shares or funds you are thinking of buying are intrinsically any good. All the best timing and psychology in the world won't rescue your money if it's tied up in dogs (see Dog).

Market-Maker

Used to be known as jobbers (see Jobber). They buy and sell shares using their own capital (or in most cases the capital of the financial conglomerate they work for). This is called risk capital. The only way market-makers can make money is to accurately anticipate the direction of the shares (or other investments such as bonds) that they are dealing in. They go 'short' – sell shares they do not own – if they think the shares are about to take a tumble or 'long' – buy shares for the book – if they think the shares are going up. These people are traders and by definition, their time horizons are short (see Trader, Trading). Whereas most of us are looking to build up an investment portfolio for the long-term (meaning three to five years), they see three to five minutes as long term. A market-maker has to be able to react in a nanosecond to good or bad news. Their eyes are always darting around, absorbing all the financial news on the various information services, which include SEAQ, Bloomberg, Reuters, Sky News, CNN, CNBC, etc, and their ears are straining to listen for hot gossip on their numerous telephones. This might explain why most of them have the attention span of a gnat.

Maturity Date

By now you have no doubt that a bond is basically an IOU, issued by a government, company or local authority to a lender. Nearly all bonds (see Bonds) have a finite lifespan, ie, the issuer sets the day on which it will repay the debt at the start of the bond's life. The day on which the bond expires and the bondholder is due to be paid back in full is called the maturity date. It is also known as the redemption date, so-called because it is the date on which the lender redeems his or her loan. There are a few bonds that are irredeemable, such as undated War Loans. The actual amount paid back to the lender is the par (or face) value of the bond, which is usually £100 (see Par Value). Insurance policies also 'mature' on the day they are fully paid up.

Mediums

Also known as medium-dated gilts, these are UK government bonds that have a lifespan of 5 to 15 years (see Bonds, Gilts, Longs, Maturity Date, Shorts).

Mergers & Acquisitions – M&A

If companies didn't like getting into bed with other companies and acquiring (as well as disposing of) them, what would happen to those sleek, pinstriped, lean and hungry corporate financiers who spend their days and nights schmoozing with company directors and poring over company accounts and legal documents in order to make sure that the transactions they're setting up for their clients will run smoothly? An M & A team (a sub-division of the corporate finance department in an investment bank) works on deals regardless of whether transactions happen or not. They get paid on results, so only earn lucrative fees when the deal they're working on comes to fruition (see Corporate Finance, Due Diligence, Investment Bank).

Mezzanine Finance

Imagine a company is like a cake. The shareholders' funds are the sponge, the borrowings are the icing, and the mezzanine debt is the marzipan in the middle. Mezzanine then, is halfway between debt and equity. It is always subordinated to ordinary debt, ie, ranking behind ordinary debt if a company goes belly up.

Investment banks typically provide this sort of financing to smaller companies that are not yet floated on the stock market or that are still growing at a rapid rate. It helps them to expand sufficiently to gain a stock market listing. Mezzanine finance carries a high-risk tag, which is why investment banks get the lion's share of the rewards for having provided it, when the company succeeds in gaining a stock market quote. Unsurprisingly, the same investment bank's corporate finance department is usually retained to organize this and gets paid big fat fees for doing so.

Mezzanine finance can also sometimes be provided as part of a large restructuring package when a company decides to (or is forced to) redesign its whole financial make-up. This kind of financing is very costly for the company because it has to pay through the nose to be given the privilege of getting (or continuing to get) the cash. About one in five mezzanine investments works out the way the bankers planned them to, so the stars have to cover the losses from the dogs!

Mid-Market Price

When stockbrokers buy and sell shares on the stock market, the market-maker's 'bid' is the price he's willing to pay for them, and his 'offer' is what he'll sell them for. The average of the two is the mid-market price, and it's the number you see when you look at share prices in the newspapers (see Bid, Offer, Spread).

Minority Interests

It's tempting to think that they are a small segment of unfairly treated members of society being protected by Islington Council, but you'd be wrong. It's just a way in which companies treat, for accounting purposes, the fact that they often own a majority stake in other companies, but not 100 per cent of them.

If you are cruising through the annual report and accounts of a company with minority interests, you will see that the small percentage of those other companies not owned by the group is put aside as 'attributable minority interests' in a separate section of the accounts, called the parent company's balance sheet. The importance of this is to ensure that the company's overall assets are not overstated.

Monetary Policy

The government borrows cash from others and us in the form of gilts. The Bank of England is responsible for setting UK interest rates and printing banknotes. All the above fall under the aegis of monetary policy (see Bank of England, Base Rate, Fiscal Policy, Gilts, Interest Rate).

Money Market

This is the market in which banks and institutions lend money to each other. Because the big cheeses put very large sums of money on deposit overnight or for short periods of time, they get much better rates of interest than we, as individuals, do. You and I can only access the money markets through unit trusts (see Unit Trust).

Money Supply

Otherwise known as M0, M1, M2, M3 and M4, this is not to be confused with Great Britain's motorways. It is the total amount of money in general circulation in the country as printed by the UK government. It includes sterling deposits with commercial banks. The numbers; 0, 1, 2, 3 and 4 refer to different ways in which the amount of money in the financial system is measured.

Monopolies & Mergers Commission – MMC

The late Screaming Lord Sutch strongly objected to the MMC on the grounds that it was a monopoly! It's a government body that checks out any company that looks as if it might be operating a monopoly against the public interest. This includes M&A deals and takeovers (see Mergers & Acquisitions – M&A, Takeover). The Monopolies & Mergers Commission checks to see whether the newly merged group will have an unfair monopoly in its line of business. Not all deals are referred to the MMC. There are set criteria that determine whether an MMC ruling is necessary or not.

Mortgage

A loan, usually from a bank or similar financial institution, to you or me for the purchase of a house. The lender will want the original capital paid back, ie, the loan itself, and interest for agreeing to lend you that lovely lolly over the lifetime of the loan. And of course, if you don't cough up, the lender will probably take your house away!

Every mortgage has just these two elements to it. The lump sum of capital borrowed and the interest paid on it, which has to be repaid to the lender over an agreed period of time. Most mortgages have a 25-year life, but in today's age of relatively low interest rates, there is an increasing trend towards more flexible mortgages, which have a longer or shorter lifespan, let you take a payment holiday, pay off lump sums in one go or pay more in some months than others, depending on how flush you are feeling. Some lenders calculate interest payable on a daily or monthly, rather than yearly rate, which can save you a lot of money. The most straightforward type of mortgage is the repayment variety – which is a daft description because all mortgages have to be repaid! Still, here goes:

Repayment Mortgage

You pay back the interest on the loan and the loan capital over the life of the mortgage. In the early years, the repayment constitutes mainly interest and not much capital – at this point you own two bricks and a window. In the later years, it will comprise more capital and less interest – you now own five bricks, a door and some roof tiles! The size of the (usually monthly) payments will vary as interest rates go up and down unless of course, you have locked in the level of interest that you pay for a period, in which case the payments will stay unchanged during that time.

Offset Mortgage

In effect this is a repayment mortgage with one important difference. Here's an example of how it works: suppose you have a £100,000 mortgage and you've got £20,000 in a savings account somewhere else. This type of mortgage combines the two accounts into one, ie, it amalgamates your savings and borrowings. As the £20,000 in savings is used to 'offset' your £100,000 mortgage, it means you only pay interest on £80,000 of the mortgage so it reduces your monthly mortgage repayments. Meanwhile you're effectively earning tax-free interest on your savings, as normally any returns on savings are taxed at source (see Composite Interest Rate). This type of mortgage is becoming increasingly popular as it's good news for those with savings as well as a mortgage.

Endowment Mortgage

If you apply for one of these, relax. The lender won't examine your vital statistics beforehand! It may seem complicated, but in fact an endowment mortgage is very straightforward. It is just like a repayment mortgage, but with one key difference. Instead of paying back the capital straight to the lender bit by bit, the borrower regularly puts this money aside into a life assurance policy called an endowment. The money in this endowment policy is invested in a fund (finance-speak – an investment plan), which ought to grow sufficiently over the long term to pay off the capital on the agreed date. Should you have the audacity to shuffle off this mortal coil before your mortgage is repaid, this type of mortgage theoretically ensures that the debt is repaid in full. Comforting thought! Of course there is a slight glitch. The money in the endowment 'investment plan' may not grow sufficiently. If you've already got this type of mortgage, it would be prudent to ask the people who supplied you with it, whether it is on track to pay off the debt. Regrettably, due to poor performance on many of these policies, most of us are better off with a straightforward repayment mortgage (see Endowment).

Other Types of Mortgage

Pension-linked and ISA mortgages all work on the same principles as an endowment mortgage, albeit they are different products. You pay the lender back the interest, while the capital is set aside into an investment plan, which is invested over the long term by you or your financial adviser. Hopefully it grows enough to pay off the 'capital' part of your mortgage in full. As with endowment mortgages, there is no guarantee that the contents of the investment plan will be enough to pay off this capital fully when it's time to pay the lender back. One final point; these types of mortgage don't offer life cover, so borrowers with families need to make sure they make provisions to protect their dependants in the event of their untimely demise.

My conclusion? There are a *huge* variety of mortgages on offer. It pays to consult a good specialist mortgage adviser for help on what's a pretty long-term commitment (see Independent Financial Adviser). The most crucial thing is to get him or her to explain very clearly the advantages and disadvantages of each type of mortgage. It's so much hassle to change things once you have signed on the dotted line that it's far better to think it over carefully and get it right first time round.

Mortgage-Backed Securities

Bonds that have been issued to investors to provide the money to lend to home-buyers.

MSCI World Index – Morgan Stanley Capital International

It's like a super-duper FTSE 100 index, only instead of tracking the fortunes of the top 100 UK companies, it does the equivalent globally, giving the biggest stock markets the most weighting. Of course, this means that the United States and Japan are the dominant forces in the index. It's useful for investors who want to have international stock market exposure outside the UK.

Multi-Manager Funds

Also called 'manager of managers', these are a relatively new type of collective fund. Basically it's when a fund manager running one fund gives chunks of the money from this fund to other external fund managers to manage. He divides the cash into several chunks, giving each chunk to a different fund manager but the money is 'segregated' so ultimately all the dosh is still safely housed under his one fund. The good news is that with this type of investment you only pay one annual management fee. The idea behind it is that the person running the 'multi-manager' fund can cherry pick from the vast array of fund managers out there so he can choose those that he thinks will deliver peak performance for investors. Also, if he is dissatisfied with one manager's performance he has the flexibility to withdraw the money pronto and hand it over to someone who he feels will do a better job (see Active Management, Diversification, Fund of Funds, Managed Funds).

Multiple

Multiple is an abbreviated City expression commonly used for things like price/earnings ratio, also called p/e multiple, and price/cash flow ratio, ie, price/cash flow multiple (see Price/Cash Flow Ratio, Price/Earnings Ratio, Price/EBITDA Ratio).

Mutual Funds

The American jargon for collective funds such as our unit trusts. These funds do just the same thing, pooling the money of many individual investors, so that it can be invested across a very wide range of assets, thus reducing the risk that something might go horribly wrong (see Collective Funds, Diversification, Managed Funds, Unit Trust).

N

Naked Option

It would be safer to run down a crowded street in broad daylight wearing no clothes than to indulge in this practice. It's one of those lovely financial phrases, along with 'butterfly strangle' and 'long straddle', that's lifted from the world of derivatives (red alert, red alert!). When an options writer goes 'naked' they are taking a massive risk; by giving someone else the right to buy shares from them or sell the shares to them, when they don't own the underlying shares or have enough money to take delivery of them from the person to whom he has sold the option (see Writer). In the belief that he is on to a winner, the writer has not bothered to protect himself by hedging (see Hedging). Should, by chance, their unswerving conviction that they are right turn out to be unswervingly wrong and the trade goes against them, they are stuffed.

This qualifies as out-and-out gambling. What makes it even scarier is that, as with futures, losses can be unlimited. I think it is best reserved for the professional traders who can afford to lose their firm's money and who generally understand the high risks involved (see Derivatives – Futures and Options).

Nap

These are 'hot' share tips recommended in the financial press or in investment newsletters sent to eager subscribers. Of course, you have to remember that by the time you get hold of these hot tips they are more like tepid, and cooling fast, because a few million others have simultaneously got hold of them. It's the same old story, 'Buyer beware – *caveat emptor*'.

Please don't whinge if a financial journalist offers share ideas that don't make a stellar trajectory. It really isn't their fault. Journalists have to produce good ideas regularly under pressure, and the truth is that there isn't a bottomless pit of good share tips. Finding sexy share performers is bloody hard work, and takes a lot of research and digging! That's why the professional fund managers charge you for their efforts. But oh, what joy when you read a small snippet of information about a company and a light bulb goes off in your head, and you discover that you've got just as much acumen at spotting a winner as the professionals! (See Newsletter.)

NASDAQ

Stands for National Association of Dealers Automated Quotation System. This is the second largest stock market in the world after the New York Stock Exchange and it, too, is American. Shares traded on NASDAQ are all bought and sold electronically over-the-counter (see Over-the-Counter – OTC). It is predominantly populated with US shares, with many of the US technology companies traded on it, but foreign shares are increasingly appearing as well. Along with Microsoft, there are at least 5,500 shares on the system. The website is: www.nasdaq.com.

National Insurance

Also called National Insurance Contributions or NICs. It's a little tax we pay to the government on top of our income tax. It goes into a huge government pot of money that pays for our faithful, creaking National Health Service and stuff like welfare and social security. Oh, and the paltry pension the state is offering us. If you are fully employed, NICs are lopped straight off your pay packet. If you're self-employed, you are supposed to cough up for these of your own volition (see Pension).

National Savings Certificates

In their unbounded generosity the UK government offers some of its National Savings products tax-free. Savings Certificates are in this category. What are they? Well, you hand over your money to National Savings who give you an account (pretty much like a deposit account) and a bit of paper called a certificate that tells you how much of your money is safely lodged there, and it then earns tax-free interest. If you go for these, be aware that the most popular are the index-linked variety, because they provide a safe route to beat inflation. These fall into the unadventurous, dull but very safe investment category.

If you are of a nervous disposition and really cannot stand the excitement of putting any of your money into the stock market, then find out more about these products from www.nationalsavings.co.uk.

National Savings Stock Register

For those of you who feel the irresistible urge to buy UK government bonds, or gilts, as they are more popularly known, this is the easiest and cheapest way to buy the ones that are already trading on the gilt market. Any post office will have the application forms. There's no minimum amount. The cost of buying gilts in this way is much cheaper than buying them through a stockbroker. The glitch with dealing so cheaply is that no one is going to hold your hand and tell you which ones are the best ones to go for. Another snag is that the buying and selling isn't instantaneous. There will be a lag time between filling out your application form to buy or sell the gilt and the deal actually being done.

Negative Equity

When your assets are worth less than your borrowings. The early 1990s are a fading memory of this phenomenon, a truly terrible time in the UK property market.

Net Asset Value - NAV

This is accounting-speak, the purpose of which is to work out the value of things owned by a company once you strip out all the money it owes. It's an easy-peasy mathematical calculation, so don't get fazed. Using the famous Bloggins plc as an example:

(Money Owed To Bloggins + Its Other Assets) – (Bloggins' Debts) = Net Asset Value

The next logical step, once you've got net asset value, is to convert it into net asset value per share (see below).

Net Asset Value per Share – NAVPS

This number gives financial whiz-kids an idea as to the value of the assets or things that back each share in a company. Most companies are valued for their earnings per share. City analysts get all hot under the collar about net asset value per share (NAV or NAVPS) when they are looking at companies that have juicy assets like land or property, or other tangible things worth money. Some specialists really relish crunching the numbers for investment trusts (ITs). These are companies listed on the Stock Exchange that just buy shares in other companies. For some reason, ITs often trade at a hefty discount to NAV. It means that the value of the assets in the company is more than the market is acknowledging. ITs can be worth buying because of this discount, but it depends on the type of assets (see Investment Trust). The maths sum that tells you net asset value per share is pretty straightforward:

$$\frac{\text{Net Asset Value}}{\text{No of Ordinary Shares in Issue}} = \text{Net Asset Value per Share}$$

Net Book Value

Accounting-speak. This is like book value, only the number is adjusted for depreciation (see Book Value, Depreciation).

Net Current Assets

Accounting-speak again. Anything in a business that can be easily and quickly converted into cash, usually within one year, to repay debts constitutes a current asset. Hey, another easy-peasy one:

Current Assets – Current Liabilities = Net Current Assets

Net Present Value

See Present Value of Money.

Neutral Weighting

If the shares held in a managed fund comprise the same proportion (known as weighting) as that of the index or benchmark to which the fund is being compared, then it means that the fund has a neutral weighting in those shares (see Managed Funds, Overweight, Underweight).

New Issue

When a company or its shareholders sell shares for the first time on the stock market, which are offered to the public – you, me and a few million others – it is a 'new issue' and the fortunate (or not so fortunate, depending on which issues we're talking about!) public get invited to subscribe for them:

1. A government-owned business is called a privatization and UK investors are offered shares in British Something or Other. In this instance you usually only get a small allocation of shares.
2. Very big companies are often offered to the public via an 'Offer for Sale' or an initial public offering called an IPO. An investment bank handles the sale of the company (see Investment Bank, Prospectus).
3. Smaller companies often favour a 'placing' because it costs them less to get listed on the Stock Exchange this way. These shares are usually sold to the big bods, ie, the institutions, via a stockbroker and are not so readily available to the general public (see Placing).

New issues don't incur commission charges or the usual stamp duty levied on share purchases. But one word of caution – just because a share is newly coming to the stock market doesn't automatically mean it's going to be a roaring success. Indeed, quite a few of the new issues listed on the stock market in recent years have been dogs (see Dog). So, to quote an oft-repeated phrase and not because I want to impress you with my very limited knowledge of Latin, '*Caveat emptor* – buyer beware!'

Newsletter

Often the financial equivalent of that illustrious newspaper, *Racing Post*, these are published on a weekly, bi-weekly or monthly basis. In them will be 'hot tips' on shares that are (allegedly) likely to surge upwards overnight. In truth, since these often involve smaller companies that are naturally more volatile, and the newsletters reach thousands of small investors, it doesn't take too many of them buying shares in a company to make the predictions self-prophesying. Still, some of them can be a useful source of information (see Nap).

New York Stock Exchange – NYSE

Sometimes called 'Noisy', sometimes called 'Nice', this is the world's largest stock market by volume of business transacted. Shares are traded electronically.

Nikkei 225 Index

Like the FTSE 100, only it measures the financial health of the 225 largest blue-chip Japanese companies listed on the Tokyo Stock Exchange. It's the one everyone looks to when they want to know how the Japanese stock market is doing (see Footsie – FTSE).

Nil-Paid Rights

This is when you have the right to own shares now but pay for them later. They are usually brought into existence in the early stages of a company's rights issue (see Partly Paid Shares, Rights Issue).

Nominal Value

When a company issues its shares, it creates a notional value for each share. This notional value is called the nominal value, and is often 10p, 50p or £1. A share's nominal value bears little or no resemblance to the price at which it is traded on the stock market. Nominal value can be changed by implementing a share split (see Share Split). It is NOT the same as par value, which describes the face value of bonds (see Par Value). Accounting enthusiasts should check out Share Premium Account.

Nominated Adviser – Nomad

Investment banks supervise and help the big companies to get on to the main Stock Exchange. But who looks after those young companies with high hopes and good ideas that are not ready to take their place on the big stock market stage yet? Nominated advisers, called 'nomads', help them to get listed on the fledgling stock market called AIM (see Alternative Investment Market – AIM). Although there are fewer rules and regulations surrounding the AIM-listing process, the onus is on the 'nomads' to make sure they only get involved with good companies or their own long-term reputations will suffer if they are seen to be promoting ropy ones.

Nominee Account

Also called a designated account. Basically, it's when a stockbroker, or a similar financial institution, sets up an account for you that will hold all your shares. It's called a nominee or designated account because it's not in your name. It is in the name of the company that has set up the account for you. However, you are the beneficial owner of the shares and obviously any dividends paid to that shareholding belong to you. Some people find the anonymity in holding shares this way appealing. Obviously it's important to make sure that whoever is holding the shares for you, ie, the intermediary, is trustworthy and passes all information and dividend payments on to you. The fly in the ointment is that nominee shareholders are not entitled to vote, receive annual reports or shareholder perks, which is a major bone of contention for many (see Shareholder Perks, Voting Shares).

Non-Marketable Securities

Also called unmarketable securities, this means you've bought them, but just you try and sell! Well, there's the thing, you can't. They're not traded on the stock market or any other kind of market for that matter, including Chapel Market or the Portobello Road. Once you've got these, you are committed. No, I don't mean you should be committed, just that you can't change your mind and unload them on to someone else. So when you buy these, you'd better make sure you want them (see Marketable Securities, Securities).

Non-Voting Shares

These shares do not entitle you to vote at a company's Annual General Meeting or at any other shareholders' meetings, for that matter (see 'A' Shares, Voting Shares).

Notes to the Accounts

This is where those of you who enjoy combing through the laborious detail of a company's affairs will have an absolute field day. By now you've whiled away a pleasant afternoon riveted by the contents of the annual report of a company in which you are interested to buy shares or bonds. You've seen that after the actual accounts, there is a section called 'Notes to the Accounts'. This is usually much longer and even more thrilling than the accounts. Leaving no stone unturned (well sometimes they – shall we say – suppress things that they're not supposed to), these offer copious explanations as to how the financial numbers were arrived at (see Accounts, Auditor, Auditor's Report).

Ofex

This is an independent market that enables very young or small companies that do not have a stock market listing to raise money, increase their profile, get a valuation and a 'trading facility' ie, a means of getting their shares traded without being quoted on AIM or the main stock market. As these companies are smaller than companies listed on AIM or the stock market, there is, by definition, a higher risk associated with investments of this kind. Its website is: www.ofex.com (see Alternative Investment Market – AIM, Quoted Company, Stock Exchange, Stock Market).

Offer

The price at which a share can be bought on the stock market (see Bid, Spread).

Offer Document

Not to be confused with a prospectus (see Prospectus). This is a very swanky-looking document issued by company A, which is bidding for company B, to the shareholders of company B. It aims to be as persuasive as possible and persuade the poor sap, I mean astute investor, to sell his or her shares and accept the offer being made by company A.

Offer For Sale

This is when a company sells its shares for the first time on the stock market and offers them to the general public and institutions. The terms 'Initial Public Offering' (IPO), 'float' and 'flotation' also mean the same thing.

Open-End Funds

These are collective funds managed by professional fund managers, which grow (or shrink) in size. Investors can pile in more and more cash, or alternatively take it out (in City-speak it's called making redemptions), hence the reason why they are given the name 'open-end' funds. The price investors pay for each of the fund's units reflects the spread, which, as for shares, is the differential between the price at which the units can be bought and sold. It also reflects the net asset value of the fund, which is fairly closely tied to the price of each unit, thus offering a certain amount of protection to the investor and the comfort of knowing that there are substantial assets backing each unit they own (see Closed-End Funds, Fund Management, Net Asset Value, Open-End Investment Company – OEIC, Spread, Unit Trust).

Open-End Investment Company – OEIC

This describes a type of unit trust (see Unit Trust). The main difference between an OEIC and a unit trust is that, with an OEIC, you buy and sell the units at one and the same price. With a unit trust, if you had to buy and sell units on the same day you would lose money because there is a difference between the price at which you can buy the units and sell them, which is called the bid/offer spread (see Spread). A relatively new type of fund in the collective fund spectrum, these are becoming increasingly popular (see Collective Funds, Managed Funds).

Options – Traditional and Traded

See Derivatives.

Ordinary Shares

See Shares.

Organisation for Economic Co-operation and Development – OECD

A group of rich countries whose main aim is to encourage each other to achieve good economic growth, improved standards of living, ensure financial stability, and a whole load of other happy-clappy altruistic aims. Much time is spent by the OECD's number crunchers trying to predict economic growth in the individual countries and the group as a whole.

Out of the Money

If you are the proud owner of a call or put option in shares (see Call Option, Derivatives – Options, Put Option), then, trust me, you will not want to exercise the option while it is 'out of the money'. Why? Because you can get a better transaction price for the shares in the stock market than that at which your call or put option has been fixed (see At the Money, In the Money). This also applies to currency options or whatever.

Outperform

When the returns of an investment exceed the returns of the bench-mark against which it is being compared (see Underperform).

Oversold

Before shares are oversold they have frequently been overbought in the first place! This term describes shares that are dumped wholesale by those who owned them previously. It often happens when a company delivers a bit of bad news, sending investors rushing for the exit door. If, in fact, the bad news was only a temporary glitch, the shares will bounce back quite rapidly. If the news is really gory, then the shares could bounce (in City-speak this is known as a 'suckers' rally' or a 'dead cat bounce') and then plummet some more.

Over-the-Counter – OTC

This describes shares and bonds bought and sold over-the-counter, ie, not through an official exchange. In the United States, the market in OTC shares is absolutely vast and it's called NASDAQ (see NASDAQ). Many of the companies with shares traded on it are huge – Bill Gates's Microsoft is one of them – and they are very well researched. Others are not followed very widely, and as there isn't so much information available to investors about them, they can be much higher-risk investments than the big 'blue chips'.

Overweight

Fund managers who binge on cream buns! In truth, it's when shares or bonds held in a fund comprise a higher proportion (known as weighting) than that of the index or benchmark to which the fund is being compared, ie, the fund is overweight in those shares, bonds, or whatever (see Neutral Weighting, Underweight).

P

Paper

A general term describing shares and bonds.

Partly-Paid Shares

When a company's shares are brought to the market in the form of a new issue, investors more often than not have to cough up for them in one hit. However, there are some new issues that allow payment for the shares to be spread over two or three instalments. The privatization of British Telecom shares in 1984 (seems a lifetime ago) offered shares to the public, to be paid for in three tranches: Nov 1984, June 1985 and Nov 1986. Total cost, £1.50 per share (see Nil-Paid Rights).

Par Value

Also called value at par. All bonds have a par (face) value. Most, but not all, bonds have a par value of £100. This is what the investor who owns them gets at the time when the borrower pays off (redeems) the bond (see Bonds, Maturity Date).

Penny Share

Amazing this. A share that's bought and sold on the stock market usually for less than a pound or just a few pennies. To the uninitiated, these may seem a bargain and incredibly good value, but in reality, of course, there is a catch. Most of them are pretty high-risk, almost like having a punt on the gee-gees. Habitual buyers of these should look upon any profits made as an unexpected bonus.

Pension

Groan. I can just see your eyes glazing over at this point. Wake up and enjoy this stimulating and mesmerizingly interesting topic! We all know the theory of a pension. It's a large wodge of money that you have built up over your working life, which is supposed to provide for you in your dotage. Come retirement, you'll be sipping Pina Coladas on the beach in the Bahamas from the carefully invested proceeds of that money. But there is a major snag – you can't access the pension until the age of 50 (this will rise to 55 from 2010).

As of 6 April 2006, the whole pension world is being turned on its head. It's such an important turning point that it's now been named 'A' Day by the financial cognoscenti. As of this date there is just one single set of rules that applies to all pensions. So it's dead simple for anyone who wants to go ahead with a new pension after that date. But for the millions who already have one, it's going to be pretty complex because we will all have to make the transition to comply with the new rules. Consult the government's website as a starting point: www.dwp.gov.uk.

Because pensions are such a long-term commitment, they need a lot of thought and are not to be entered into lightly. It makes sense to enlist a good independent financial adviser to guide you through the maze and explain your options. Make sure you go through the pros and cons of the myriad different pension plans on offer (see Independent Financial Adviser – IFA).

Should we buy a pension at all? Well, the government makes it almost irresistible to do so by offering full tax relief on contributions (see Tax Relief). The funds in the plan also grow tax-free. Rather than pontificate endlessly about this, I thought it best to simply lay out below the choice of pensions open to us.

State Benefits

Everyone who is fully employed is entitled to get state benefits at retirement, via National Insurance contributions, otherwise called

NICs (see National Insurance). There's the Old Age Pension, which most people get eventually, if they live long enough. Then there's a top-up pension called SERPS (State Earnings Related Pension Scheme), which has been replaced by the State Second Pension (S2P). The amount of the top-up varies depending on your salary and work history.

The new S2P is 'pay as you go' and is likely to be drastically cut back in the future. This effectively means that anyone earning more than £9,000 a year will have to get their own private pension. Basically, you're on your own mate! Everybody who is entitled to the S2P top-up is equally at liberty to opt out of state benefits and direct their NICs towards their own personal pension plan.

The government introduced a new personal pension plan called a Stakeholder Pension back in 2001. This has had the positive effect of forcing down the cost of pensions and is a very cost-effective way of buying one. All employers now have to provide a stake-holder for their employees. They won't have to make contributions to it, but they will have to run it on the employee's behalf. The government continues to put pressure on pension providers to lower the costs of personal pensions and make them more easy to understand. This has to be good news!

Company Pensions

Let's tackle all you fully employed folk. This is easy. Nine times out of ten, you're better off in your company pension plan. Phew, breathe a sigh of relief; no need to think any further. All you have to decide is whether you want to top it up with an AVC or not (see Additional Voluntary Contributions – AVC below). You've prob-ably already sussed that company pension schemes are better than personal pensions because with the former, the company makes contributions to it on your behalf.

There are only two types of company pension (otherwise called occupational pensions): final salary and money purchase. The final salary is the optimum, but don't turn your nose up at the slightly less advantageous money purchase variety. However, the only option available for self-employed folk, or employees without company pension schemes, is to go for a personal pension.

Final Salary Pension

Also runs under the confusing title of 'defined benefits scheme'. With this type of pension what you get on retirement depends on three things: 1) your final salary level; 2) how many years' service you've put in; and 3) the rate of accrual your employer gives you for every year you have worked for the company. Take an easy example: if you retire, having worked ten years for a company that is paying you 1/60 of your final salary per year, you'll get 10/60 or 1/6 of your final salary. The maximum you can get is 1/30 of your final salary per year of service. The more common version is 1/60. This is by far the best type of pension you can get, and, if you've got one, you are definitely laughing.

Money Purchase Pension

Also called a 'defined contributions scheme'. Jeepers-creepers, it's as if they don't want us to get a pension at all, given the jargon-loaded phrases they use! This can be a company or personal pension scheme. With the company variety, you and your employer make contributions to the pension, which are invested on your behalf in the company's name. The fund of money grows tax-free, and when you retire, you get the proceeds, which have hopefully increased substantially over the years. However, while a final salary pension guarantees you a proportion of your salary, no matter what, you don't get the same assurance with a money purchase one. With this, what you get depends on how well the fund has grown and the level of annuity rates when you retire. Whilst the money purchase isn't quite as attractive as the final salary, both are usually a better bet than having solely to fund your own personal pension.

Personal Pension

For those of us not fortunate enough to be offered a good company scheme, the only alternative is to go out there and buy a personal pension, which is portable between jobs.

Self-Invested Personal Pension – SIPP

Now these are seriously good news for those who get enlightened about them. Most commonly called a SIPP, this kind of does what it says on the tin. It's a personal pension, which is a tax-free container that you have to take out with a SIPP provider. You, as the owner of the SIPP, can put your money into any investment as long as pension rules allow it. You can choose what assets are bought or sold, and when they are bought or sold. The bad news is that, as of 6 April 2006, ie, the first day in the new tax year (also known as 'A' Day in the industry), SIPPs can only contain commercial property, not residential, as previously mooted by the government. Anyone considering buying commercial property for a SIPP needs specialist advice because there are all sorts of implications to popping property into one, and doing this won't suit everybody. A good independent financial adviser will take the headache out of deciding whether this is the right type of pension for you.

Pension Annuity

Did someone mention nudity? Oh, annuity! A very large chunk of the money we save in a pension plan is used, on retirement, to buy us a secure annual income for life called an annuity. Historically, government law hasn't allowed us to take all that lovely loot as one lump sum. Talk about spoiling our fun! Maybe it doesn't trust us to spend it wisely. Whilst we have the good fortune to live longer than we used to, the result is that, together with the long-term drop in interest rates, annuity rates have been steadily falling in recent times. Unless there is a dramatic rise in interest rates we are unlikely to see an improvement in the situation. Many annuities look pretty paltry; so what's the answer?

Don't fall off your chair but there is some good news. After 'A' Day, ie, 6 April 2006, we still can't take all the money out of our pension in a lump sum (shame!). However, whilst you can still take out an annuity from your pension, which means buying it all in one go on retirement as before, there is now the additional option of being able to use your pension to draw an income from the fund throughout your life. This makes it more flexible.

If you opt for an annuity, don't forget that there's no obligation to take it from the firm that's supplied your pension. You can shop around and look for the sexiest annuity rates, using a good IFA or specialist annuity broker.

In truth, this whole area is so complex it really needs specialist expert advice; a good IFA can help you through the maze (see Independent Financial Adviser).

Additional Voluntary Contributions – AVC

An AVC is like an extension to your occupational (ie, work) pension. If you have a pension scheme you can choose to top it up with your own money. This means making AVCs – added voluntary contributions – to it so that you get more income during your retirement. Like pensions, AVCs are a tax-effective way of saving and are eventually paid out as a regular monthly income or lump sum. The only snag with these is that you cannot get access to the funds until you retire.

An in-house AVC is one set up by your employer and is normally subject to the main rules of the company's pension scheme. A free-standing AVC is totally separate from your main pension scheme. Should you change jobs, you can take it with you. It is also confidential from employers. One advantage is that you can choose where the funds are invested. However, a major disadvantage with these is that they are more costly than in-house AVCs, which benefit from economies of scale.

Permanent Income-Bearing Shares – PIBS

These are not shares, as the title seems to suggest. They are in fact bonds issued by building societies (see Bonds). Like other bonds, they are tradable and can be bought and sold via a stockbroker. And like other bonds traded on the market, the price of these can go up as well as down, so they are not necessarily totally 'safe' places to put money just because they come from a building society. PIBS make a twice-yearly pre-agreed interest payment to their holders. As they are irredeemable, ie, the loan is never paid back, this interest is paid *ad infinitum* (see Maturity Date).

Placing

When a stockbroking firm, or several of them, have a large line of shares to sell, and sell it directly to institutional investors, it is known as a placing. As a private investor, you won't get the benefit of this – only in an indirect sense, as those shares often go into pension and life insurance funds.

Poison Pill

This is the term used to describe tactics used by companies that strongly object to being taken over by other companies. The company being bid for will do its damndest to swallow a 'poison pill'; one way might be acquiring another company to make it look less attractive to the marauding bidder trying to take it over. Alternatively, it could find a legal technicality that would prevent a takeover, or take on board a truck load of very unappealing debt! Naturally in any bid situation, shareholders get pretty excited because, nine times out of ten, they're quids in whatever happens (see Asset Stripper, White Knight).

Portfolio

A group or a range of assets owned by one person or a company. You, for example, might own a house and some shares and a bar of gold. This is a portfolio of assets. It's a term often applied to a range of investments such as shares and bonds (see Diversification, Portfolio Management).

Portfolio Management

Anybody can manage a portfolio for him or herself. You can own a group of shares and that's classed as a portfolio. What you or I cannot do is manage a portfolio for others unless we are authorized to do so. Before people can get their mitts on our cash, you'll be relieved to know that they need a number of pretty high-powered qualifications and special authorization to do so. Only then can you safely hand it over to them. They are generally called fund managers (see Financial Services Authority, Fund Management).

Pre-emption Rights

When a company needs to raise cash via the stock market, its existing shareholders are given the right to purchase any new shares it might issue. This stops their share being diluted to less than the original percentage they owned. It is called giving those existing shareholders pre-emption rights. If they decide not to take up their rights, the rights themselves are traded on the stock market, which gives outside investors the opportunity to purchase them in order to buy into the shares (see Dilution, Nil-Paid Rights, Rights Issue).

Preference Shares

Here, the term share is a bit misleading. Preference shares are not like ordinary shares, or 'equity'. They are actually more like bonds in that they almost always offer a fixed return, also known as a dividend. This contrasts with ordinary shares, which may or may not pay out a dividend, depending on how well a company is doing. The good news is that 'prefs', as they are commonly known, rank ahead of ordinary shares in terms of dividend payout. And in a worst case scenario, should a company go belly up, preference shareholders will be paid out before ordinary shareholders. The bad news is that although these shares are arguably less risky and 'safer' than ordinary shares, investors in these will miss out on any good news and capital appreciation that the ordinary shares might achieve. And if the company runs into a rough patch, it can waive the dividend payout to preference shareholders as well as to its ordinary shareholders. To discover the order of payout in the event of a company going bust, see Shares.

Preliminary Announcement

A company makes one of these two or three months after the end of its financial year. They'll announce what wonderful profits (or losses) they've racked up, how much they owe in taxes and what they intend to pay to you, dear investor, by way of dividend. The Stock Exchange gets first notification of the 'prelims', followed by the press. Most of us only find out the results from the newspapers the following morning, by which time the City analysts will have long got hold of them and be furiously crunching away at the numbers in order to get on to their big clients and give their opinions as to whether things look rosy or bleak for the company.

Premium

Basically means the difference between the price of something and its 'real' underlying value. An example is when shares are issued on the stock market in the form of a new issue. If the shares, once they are traded, rise above the level at which they were originally priced, they are said to be at a premium.

Premium is also the word used to describe the money you pay when you buy options, rather like insurance premiums (see Call Option, Put Option, Derivatives – Options). And, of course, it also means the money insurance companies extract from us on a regular basis.

Premium Bonds

These bonds are vigorously promoted as a tax-free investment. But there is a major catch. The interest your money earns on the bonds is pooled with the interest earned by all the other 'investors' and distributed in the form of monthly prizes from a computerized draw to the lucky few. Most of the poor saps that own premium bonds get nothing, that's *niente*, *nada*, *nichts*, diddly, zilch.

Present Value of Money

The value now of money that is to be received in the future. It often describes the stream of income you might expect to get over several years from an investment. The City whiz-kids use a complicated mathematical calculation called 'discounted cash flow' to work out the present value of money. This enables them to price the investments (see Discounted Cash Flow).

Price/Cash Flow Ratio

The price/cash flow of a company is worked out in the same way as a price/earnings ratio:

$$\frac{\text{Share Price}}{\text{Cash Flow per Share}} = \text{Price/Cash Flow Ratio}$$

Although price/cash flow is clearly not as good a measure of a company's profitability as its price/earnings ration, what it does do is enable the number crunchers to make international comparisons between the shares of companies as it eliminates all the different accounting practices used in various countries (see Cash Flow, Price/Earnings Ratio).

Price/Earnings Ratio – P/E

Also known as the p/e ratio, price/earnings multiple, earnings multiple, p/e multiple, or just multiple, which can get confusing to the uninitiated. But it's very simple, I promise! It's just another basic maths calculation:

$$\frac{\text{Share Price}}{\text{Earnings per Share}} = \text{Price/Earnings Ratio}$$

The number you get is a clue that tells you what the market is expecting of this share in terms of future price performance. The City bods obsess over the prospective (future) p/e of a company. When a share is on a high multiple, it means that the stock market has great expectations of a company. The City expects it to exhibit fast growth and a stellar trajectory. A low multiple can mean it's either a dog (see Dog), growth within the company is pretty sluggish and the shares are not likely to go great guns, or the City has missed the virtues of the shares, which are due to be re-rated upwards. But let us be clear on one thing. The market can and does often get it wrong. Also bear in mind that a p/e ratio is only one of many tools used by the professionals to establish the value of a share. It is by no means the be-all and end-all. A low p/e number taken in isolation doesn't automatically mean that a company's shares are good value. There could be very good reasons why the shares are cheap. Certain types of company, like asset-based property ones for example, can't be sussed out using a p/e ratio. Don't get me wrong; it's a useful number just as long as it is taken in context with all the other info about a company (see Price/Cash Flow Ratio, Price/EBITDA Ratio).

Price/EBITDA Ratio

Exactly the same as p/e ratio (see Price/Earnings Ratio). The only difference is that the earnings number is taken 'before interest, tax, depreciation and amortization'. The reason many City analysts use this figure is not because they like to make things as complicated and incomprehensible as possible, although you might think that. No, it is simply to iron out accounting differences between companies in different countries. Using a price/EBITDA ratio just means analysts can make meaningful comparisons between companies. For example, if one company depreciates its assets faster than another does, then it is better to look at earnings before depreciation (see Amortization, Depreciation).

Primary Market

When shares or bonds are offered on the stock market for the very first time (like a virgin) they are known as 'primary market' offerings (see Secondary Market).

Prime Rate

The American phrase meaning base rate (see Base Rate, Central Bank, Interest Rate).

Principal

When you act as principal in a transaction (especially when buying something) you risk your own capital. In the City it's the term often applied to traders, market-makers and stockbrokers who buy shares for their own 'book'. Naturally they do so with a view to making a profit, but it is pretty risky stuff, because they can (and do) get it wrong! When they make money it's big money, but the converse it true when they lose it (see Jobber, Market-Maker, Trader).

Private Equity

This fancy phrase describes investors in companies that aren't quoted on any stock market. They like to keep their affairs private as the name suggests. The companies they invest in are usually developed mature businesses with strong cash flows, which means banks can also lend money for the deal, ie, the purchase of the company. There are also venture capital trusts that invest in private equity (see Venture Capital, Venture Capital Trust).

Privatization

The floating of previously state-owned utilities and industries on the stock market. Initiated by the Conservatives in the early 1980s, one of the consequences was that it made millions of us into share owners. Long-term holders of these shares will have made a pretty packet by now, so who's complaining?

Profit and Loss Account

This scintillating and vitally important bit of information tells you how much money a company is making. City analysts have raptures or cold sweats poring over every little scrap of information that appears in this section of a company's accounts. It tells you how much the company sold (sales, turnover, revenue all mean the same thing), how much it cost to make those sales, and the overall expenses to the company of things like tax and dividend payouts. Then, if they are really lucky, there might be some retained profits left over that can be ploughed back into the company.

Make sure you look at the numbers in the consolidated profit and loss account, not that of its parent. Consolidated just means that the numbers are adjusted to include the correct percentage of all the businesses part or wholly belonging to the company (see Accounts).

Prospectus

A glossy fat brochure full of a dazzling array of all the facts and figures that you will ever need to know about a company, if not more. Its purpose is to act as a reassuring, confidence-inspiring document that persuades investors to part with their hard-earned cash and invest in the company that is about to be brought to the stock market, usually in the form of a new issue or public offering. Naturally the prospectus will be upbeat and positive and designed to show the company in the best possible light. There'll be a whole bunch of numbers that make positive projections for the company's future profits and expansion, blah, blah, blah. From your point of view, one of the main things to watch for is sentiment (see Market Influences). Does the market await this new issue with baited breath, or will it be a dead duck? If you're planning on going for a new issue, financial press comment and a reliable stockbroker will help you to gauge whether to do so or not. By the way, a prospectus is not the same as an offer document (see Offer Document).

Protectionism

Something Japan has been getting away with for years. Basically it's when a country says it's not going to buy foreign imported rubbish and makes it impossible for importers to infiltrate their economy. How? It does so by setting unreasonably high tariffs, restricting the amount of goods they'll allow in, and coming up with specifications that are prohibitively expensive for the importers to meet; that sort of thing.

Provisions

A company has to make provisions for potential bad debts and depreciation; these are found in its annual report and accounts. A provision can be a warning to investors of a large looming bad thing that may well cost the company several million pounds. Alternatively, it could just be that it is being prudent and keeping money aside as a safety cushion for unexpected happenings.

Proxy

When you buy ordinary shares in a company, you are entitled to vote at its Annual General Meeting (AGM) and any Extraordinary General Meeting (EGM). Voting can be important if it involves the takeover of another company or a key issue regarding the company's finances. If you cannot make it to the AGM or EGM, you can elect someone else, ie, a proxy, to vote on your behalf, according to your instructions (see Annual General Meeting, Extraordinary General Meeting).

Public Limited Company - PLC

All companies listed on the stock market have to be plcs. Not all plcs are quoted on the stock market by any means. Many more are privately owned. The point is that a plc has more stringent accounting requirements than a non-plc. You'll see this written sometimes as PLC, other times plc.

Public Sector Borrowing Requirement - PSBR

A very grand-sounding phrase that basically means the government is strapped for cash, having spent too much (what's new?), and now needs to borrow money on a big scale, to the tune of billions of pounds. Puts my paltry overdraft to shame. Anything I can do, the government can do better! (See Monetary Policy.)

Put Option

The right, but not the obligation, to sell a share (or any other financial instrument) within a defined period of time in the future, at a price that is fixed now (see Call Option, Derivatives – Options).

Q

Quality of Earnings

Analysts like to emphasize that it's not enough if a company's earnings are growing; they have to be good quality, ie, consistent. An example: a company that has a fixed contract with a customer for 20 years will be judged by the City to have higher quality of earnings than those of a company that has short-term contracts that need to be renewed, say, every six months (see Analyst, Earnings per Share).

Quantitative Funds/Fund Management

Called 'quant' for short, it's a method of investing money that originated in the United States (naturally). Investment experts feed a whole bunch of information and numbers about stock markets and individual companies into a computer program. They then set criteria that allow it to effectively decide where the money being managed would be best invested, in geographical and risk-reward terms. The computer program is invariably incredibly complicated and scientific, and something that neither you nor I (and I suspect sometimes even the fund manager him or herself!) could possibly make head or tail of. And hey, it very often works. But there are potentially large pitfalls with this sort of fund management. The judgements made by the computer about the future are all based on an objective analysis of the past. It ignores the human element; for example, the effect that a company's management can have in turning things around in the future. It also lacks the ability to react

quickly enough to bolt-from-the-blue scenarios, ie, when something completely unexpected happens that the computer couldn't
have possibly anticipated. So there is a danger that these funds can
be too inflexible. On the occasions when things do go wrong,
investors have been known to really lose their shirts. But it just
reinforces the old, old motto, 'Thou shalt not put all thy eggs into
one basket!'

Quote

A share's 'quote' is its current price. It is normally listed on the
Stock Exchange, with its buy and sell price 'quoted' by market-
makers (see Market-Maker).

Quoted Company

Means the company is listed on the Stock Exchange. Other expressions meaning the same thing are: publicly listed company, publicly quoted company (see Quote).

R

Ramp

Beware shares that are ramped by the City bods. It happens more frequently than you think and is not always very obvious. Basically when City dealers want to get rid of some slightly dodgy shares that some other wise guys originally suckered them into, a small select band of them 'ramp' the shares by stretching the truth enormously as to their merits, just enough so that the unsuspecting investor (imagine an innocent guppy fish being circled by a shark!) will swallow the story. Curiously, as soon as the inflated or 'ramped' shares are offloaded, they have a tendency to collapse in a heap on to the heads of the poor sods who bought them.

Random Walk Theory

I feel like a random walk today – should I try Hyde Park or Kensington Gardens, I wonder. Seriously, it is a theory. Yes, that's right, a theory that has been devised by random walk theorists. Basically they reckon that, because share price movements are random, there's absolutely no point in trying to second guess, or predict, their future price movements. This puts paid to the technical analyst's theory that you can, indeed, second guess the future by looking at past share price movements (see Efficient Market Theory, Technical Analysis).

Ratios

Sums. Shriek in horror remembering all that eye-glazing algebra we had to learn at school. But it's not that bad. A ratio is simply the division of one number into another. City analysts and investors often pluck the numbers for ratios from the balance sheet and profit and loss statement of a company's accounts. These accounting ratios can give them lots of clues about the financial health or prospects for a company.

I say 'can' as opposed to 'do', because the numbers crunched by the City people are only as good as the information they glean from the management of the companies they follow. Some companies are more forthcoming than others. Anyway, serious investors set great store by these ratios, especially the analysts who make it their business to create and analyse these numbers *ad infinitum* (see Acid Test, Analyst, Price/Earnings Ratio).

Real Return

When financial whizzos talk about real returns on your money as opposed to unreal, what they actually mean is that they have stripped out inflation, which whilst unreal, feels bloody real to us when our pay packets don't keep up with it, and buy us less and less as the years go by. So to take an easy example: if the building society or bank is paying you 5 per cent on money deposited, and inflation is 2 per cent, the real return on your money is a mere 3 per cent.

Real-Time

What, as opposed to fake-time? This describes financial information transmitted 'live' as you see it. An example is the FTSE 100 index, which is calculated and recalculated every few seconds, thus displaying 'real-time' prices.

Receiver

Oh dear, oh dear, let's pray you never see one of these, because, as the word implies, it's they who will be doing the receiving, not you! When a business goes bankrupt, or sometimes even before then, people called receivers are appointed to scoop up as many of the assets remaining in that business's possession as possible, with a view to flogging them off to clear their debts (see Bankrupt, Liquidation, Shares).

Recession

Trust economists to come up with a confusing word for what is in fact very simple. The official definition of recession is 'two successive quarters of negative economic expansion'. What they actually mean is six months when the economy just doesn't grow. And how on earth can you have negative expansion, for goodness' sake?

Recovery Stocks

Some companies can sink to their knees quite quickly if things go wrong for them such as losing an important customer, or if the management is lousy. Perhaps a business is doing well, but money isn't coming in quickly enough, or it could be sensitive to changes in the general economic outlook for its products, ie, the business is cyclical (see Cyclical Shares). Regrettably, companies listed on the Stock Exchange are frequently subject to the short-termism of City analysts. As soon as they get a whiff that all is not well, they cheerfully (or not so cheerfully if they're nursing a loss!) dump the shares *en masse*. But then a few months later, the outlook might have improved for the company: it may have formed an alliance with a major customer, or it is subject to a takeover bid, or quite simply the bad management has been replaced by good. Lo and behold, as soon as there is just the tiniest glimpse of recovery in the company's fortunes, the same people who told you those shares were an unmitigated disaster and not to be touched with a bargepole, will be busily buying them up again and the company's share price may well recover sharply. That's why shares that fall and then rise rapidly are called recovery shares.

Redemption/Redemption Date

See Maturity Date.

Redemption Value

This is the amount of money that issuers of bonds, loans, etc repay to lenders on the redemption date of the loans (see Maturity Date). This value is fixed when the loan is issued.

Redemption Yield

Other phrases meaning the same thing are: 'total yield at redemption' or 'projected total yield'. Don't panic. It is just the result of a maths calculation worked out by the City types who specialize in selling bonds to investors. 'Redemption yield' is useful because it gives the investor a guide to his total returns if he decides to hang on to a bond until its redemption date (see Maturity Date). This fairly complicated calculation adds up the yearly income stream that a bond is due to pay out over its lifetime, including any capital gains or losses that will be returned to the lender at the end of its life (see Bonds, Income Yield, Running Yield, Yield).

Registered Securities

These are shares or bonds with a centralized register in which all the names of the owners, as at any moment in time, are recorded. The type that do not have such a register are called bearer securities, hence are anonymous (see Bearer Securities, Securities).

Registrar

It's the thrilling task of the registrar of a company to keep its share ownership list up to date. A registrar can be an individual, or an organization hired by a company to do this tedious, but necessary task. As millions of us buy and sell shares in various companies, there is a busy little registrar, adding and deleting our names from the share registers of those companies. They do all the other thankless tasks for which we should be grateful, like sending us our dividends, tax vouchers and notice of bonus (freebie share) issues.

Regular Savings Plan/Scheme

If you haven't been lucky enough to win the lottery, marry a millionaire, or inherit a large wodge of cash, then you should definitely think about having one of these. It involves setting aside the increasingly paltry sum of, say, £50–100 per month, into a savings plan with a view to slowly and carefully investing it into stock market pooled investment funds of your choice over a period of years. For many people who don't have huge wads of spare cash, it's a convenient way of investing because it spreads risk and saves them worrying about the close-up, day-to-day participation needed for direct share market investment. The beauty of putting in small regular sums is that it irons out the highs and lows of stock market fluctuations (see Diversification, Drip Feeding, Investment Trust, Managed Funds, Unit Trust).

Reinsurance

Insurers who offer to insure really big, mega-expensive things like oil rigs, ships or aeroplanes, worry that things might go wrong. The Piper Alpha oil rig disaster springs to mind. So to hedge their bets, they take out insurance on the things that they have agreed to insure, to minimize the necessity of having to cough up if things should go horribly wrong. They offload the risk on to another insurer, who then offloads the risk on to some other poor punter. As this process continues and each insurer successively offloads the risk of say, another oilrig blowing up, there is a real danger that things go full circle and the first insurer has regained the risk they originally tried to offload.

Relative Strength

This is when you check out the performance of an individual share against the overall stock market's performance. A popular measure in the United Kingdom is the FTSE 100. So if the FTSE 100 is up 10 per cent over a one-month period, and Gotcha plc is up 12 per cent in the same period, then Gotcha has outperformed the FTSE 100 by 2 per cent (see Outperform, Underperform).

Research

Research is the endless reams and reams of written analysis produced by City analysts on specific companies, sectors of commerce and industry, and on entire markets. The vast quantity of this stuff churned out by them rarely reaches the likes of you and me. It's reserved for the big bods, ie, the institutions (see Institutional Investors). They, being heavy hitters who can move share markets with their sheer volume of business, get the de luxe treatment. Smaller investors have to rely on the financial press and private client stockbroker research. Bear in mind that not many private client stockbrokers provide comprehensive research coverage of the whole UK stock market. Many of them tend to specialize and be very good at certain sectors, but not so good in others. PS. The advent of the internet is making stock market research more and more accessible (see Financial Information).

Reserves

There are two meanings for this in a financial sense: 1) Economic-speak – just as you and I keep some spare cash in the kitty for emergencies, governments do, too. And they like to hold the reserves of their country in a suitably stable currency (if there are any left!) such as the US dollar, preferring to steer clear of the Indian rupee or Russian rouble. 2) Accounting-speak – reserves in a company's accounts. In this context they are assets, like cash, and are shown in the balance sheet of the accounts (see Capital and Reserves).

Retail Price Index – RPI

This is one way in which our beloved UK government measures inflation. It's compiled monthly by the government statistics department. It is supposed to measure the change in prices of consumer goods and services in retail shops: stuff like clothes, food, mortgages, cars, etc. The City watches the RPI like a hawk to spot changes in trends. Any signs of an increase and they are all of a panic, fretting that with a resurgence of inflation, interest rates will have to rise to dampen it down. And if the numbers are falling, jubilation and glee set in as they eagerly anticipate a fall in interest rates. But then doom and gloom come along, as worries about an excessive fall in inflation leading to deflation set in (see Deflation, Inflation, Lagging Indicator, Leading Indicator).

Retained Earnings

When a company makes profits, it doesn't usually generously dish out all of these profits in one go to its shareholders in the form of dividends. Why not? you cry petulantly, we want more dividends. Well, the reason why not is because the company holds back some of its profits in order to have money in the kitty to grow and invest in the business, and what it holds back are called retained earnings or retained profit.

Return on Capital Employed – ROCE

Return on capital employed, you'll be thrilled to know, is one of the really useful City sums. It measures a company's ability to generate profits on its assets. The idea behind it is to see how efficiently the money in the business is being used, ie, how much profit is being squeezed out compared with each pound employed (see Capital Employed). Let's say a business is using capital of a million pounds and is generating profits of £100,000:

$$\frac{£100,000}{£1,000,000} \times 100 = \text{ROCE of } 10\%$$

Return on Equity – ROE

It's yet another ratio that the City analysts love to calculate and it tells the shareholders of the business how much profit is being generated by its total amount of funds:

$$\frac{\text{Profit Attributable to Shareholders}}{\text{Shareholders' Funds}} \times 100 = \text{Return on Equity (\%)}$$

It is a similar, but different calculation to return on capital employed, which measures how much profit is being generated from the assets at the company's disposal (see Return on Capital Employed).

Revenue

This is accounting-speak for the amount of sales or turnover generated by a business. It pops up in a company's profit and loss statement, as well as in its cash-flow statement (see Accounts, Cash-Flow Statement, Turnover).

Reverse Takeover

Confusingly, this actually means a little company swallowing up a big company. Imagine a goldfish gobbling up a river pike. It happens when a small company with very good management is able to borrow money to buy the bigger company and do better with it.

Reverse Yield Gap

Gee. I'll try not to addle your brain with this one! First thing's first. Let's start with the yield gap. In theory, shares should give a greater return than UK government bonds, ie, gilts, because they are more risky than gilts, which are effectively risk-free. Therefore shares should pay you more to compensate for that extra risk. And the difference between the return offered by gilts and the higher return offered by shares is called the yield gap. Don't ask why!

Sometimes, when the government is desperate to raise cash, it offers a higher return on gilts than that offered by shares. The differential between returns on shares and those on gilts is then called the reverse yield gap (see Gilt/Equity Ratio).

Rights Issue

When a company decides to raise more cash in order to do sensible things (we hope) to help increase its profits, one of the methods by which it can raise cash is to have a rights issue. This means they write to their shareholders and say, 'Hey guys, guess what? We really need some more money from you. But it's for a very good cause. We're going to expand our widget-producing capabilities... ' and as your eyes glaze over at the sheer tedium of it all, you notice a little word on the document: 'discount'. It jolts you into feverish excitement. Ooh, you think, I'm going to get something cheaper than usual; yippee, this must be good news. What the company has done to lure you to part with more cash is to offer you new shares at a discount. The shares are offered in direct proportion to the amount you already own. You are given a certain time period in which to take up the offer, and if you choose not to partake of it, then you can sell your rights through a stockbroker. Only, if you do decide to sell the rights, be aware that your shareholding will be diluted, ie, made smaller in comparison with the new increased amount of shares the company will then have in issue. And shares have a tendency to fall in price (in the short term) on the news that there is going to be a rights issue (see Cum-Rights, Dilution, Ex-Rights, Nil-Paid Rights).

Risk

What we take just by getting out of bed every morning! Whenever you see the cute little caveat that 'The value of your investments may go down as well as up', you know you have departed from safe, but dull-as-ditchwater building society or bank deposit territory, and are about to embark on the exciting, but undoubtedly riskier terrain of shares, bonds, unit trusts, etc. Yes, you guessed it, the better the return you expect on your money, the riskier it is.

This is an unfailing rule of investment that all too many people forget when they get carried away in the euphoria of investing their hard-earned cash. There's something about buying shares that sets people alight, as if they were at the Derby. I implore you to take a deep breath, hold back, and examine the sort of things you invest your money in as closely as you can. Try not to get too emotional and carried away with the thrill of it all. Successful investors, both large and small, never fall in love with their investments. They have a sense of detachment and are willing to bail out as soon as they see they have made a mistake. And remember a lot of it is common sense.

If you, like me, are of a cautious disposition by nature, then you'll be looking for investments that are good, solid, safe bets over the long term. So buying shares or bonds in an obscure Venezuelan computer manufacturer is not likely to be your thing. Cautious investors tend to stick to familiar home ground, buying shares in well-known companies like, for example, those that populate the FTSE 100.

Risk Premium

When investors put their money into investments such as shares or corporate bonds which are not risk-free, they expect to get a better return than they would get if they were to put the money into the effectively risk-free world of gilts (UK government bonds). So if risk-free investments offer, say, 4 per cent, investors might expect 7 or 8 per cent on a less safe investment. In this instance, the amount of return investors expect above the risk-free rate of 4 per cent is 3 per cent, also known as the risk premium (see Bonds, Gilts, Risk, Risk/Reward Ratio, Shares).

Risk/Reward Ratio

Mega-important to read this and tattoo the concept on to your forehead. Somewhere along the line, people often forget that there is a mathematical rule about the risk/reward ratio. The higher the reward you want to get, ie, the more money you want to receive back on your original outlay, the higher the risk you are taking with your hard-earned cash. There is absolutely no escaping this golden rule, and I pity the poor person who, eternally optimistic, buys into the dream that he or she can make superior returns to what banks and building societies are offering, without higher risk (see Risk).

Rumour

Something the City thrives on. And which you, sensible, unflappable person that you are, will not respond to. I have found, from experience, that it is best to be highly allergic to rumours and gossip generated from the City. Investors should only respond if they can back it up with a profound conviction that the shares in question are worth buying or have to be sold. Otherwise it could just be a ramp or a bear raid being perpetrated by the traders, gleefully watching all the small, unsuspecting punters, ie, you and me, being railroaded in or out of shares. Of course, if it's bad news and the company in which you own shares is about to hit the deck, you will be last in the queue to know about it. And if it's potentially good news, well, the same applies – by the time you find out about it, the shares will have risen at least halfway to their target price (see Bear Raid, Ramp).

Running Yield

Another delightful bit of financial jargonese that sounds very complicated, but isn't. So there's no need to get fazed. It's just the mathematical calculation that works out the return offered by a bond when its price on the market is higher or lower than its face value of £100. If the bond is selling at less than £100, the running yield will be higher than the nominal yield, ie, the return it offers when it is priced at £100, and vice versa. This is the actual, or real yield of the bond (see Bonds, Par Value, Redemption Yield, Yield).

Russell 2000

This is a popular index that measures the financial health of the
2000 smaller American companies that are next in size after the top
1000 listed on the US stock market (see Index).

S

Save As You Earn – SAYE

The lucky employee contributes money to the scheme over a number of years, which can be topped up by the employer. When the time's up, he or she gets a tax-free bonus (whoopee!) and can buy shares in the company at a pre-agreed fixed price. Anyone who is offered this option usually finds they're on to a good thing, unless the company they work for is about to go up the creek, in which case, being a shareholder isn't such a hot idea. This is similar to an Employee Share Option Plan, but not exactly the same (see Employee Share Option Plan – ESOP).

Scrip Issue

Yippee. Freebie shares to add to your existing shareholding. There are two types: 1) Scrip shares given when a company pays dividends to shareholders in the form of shares instead of cash. 2) Scrip is also another name for a bonus issue (see Bonus Issue).

Secondary Market

When shares and bonds have been issued and are already being traded publicly on the stock market, it is known as 'secondary market' dealings. The original issue of shares or bonds takes place in the 'primary market' (see Primary Market).

Sector

The UK stock market is made up of roughly 3,000 companies. To make it easier for the professionals and everybody else to follow the fortunes of these companies, they are grouped into types, or sectors. The different sectors are analysed avidly and continuously by City analysts and the financial press. There are at least 40 of them covered in the *Financial Times*, so if you're planning to follow the stock market more closely, make sure you familiarize yourself with these. You'll need a dose of the water sector after starting at alcoholic beverages (always a good place to begin!), by which time you'll be in transports of delight perusing transport shares. This sector grouping helps the City professionals and you to make comparisons between the companies, ie, suss out what's a good share to buy and hold, as well as what to avoid like the plague.

Secured Loan Stock

When you lend money to a company, if it's in the form of secured loan stock, you can sleep sounder at night. Loan stock (a bond), remember, just describes the bit of paper, the IOU these people give you in return for borrowing your cash. That magical word 'secured' conveys a comfortable, secure feeling, doesn't it? For once in the financial world, it's justified. This type of loan is secured against some valuable asset of the company, like a building, land or bars of gold. In the event of a worst case scenario, should the company have the misfortune to go belly up, secured loan stock will be repaid before unsecured loan stock (see Bonds, Corporate Bonds, Shares for a list of how debt repayments are prioritized in the event of a bankruptcy, Subordinated Loan Stock, Unsecured Loan Stock).

Securities

This is a pretty confusing word that describes a large number of things that are not necessarily secure, in the peace-of-mind sense. It is the general word that is used to describe the whole gamut of financial assets, such as shares, bonds, debentures, gilts, unit trusts, etc. Just for your information, insurance policies are not included (see Bearer Securities, Financial Instrument, Marketable Securities, Registered Securities, Non-Marketable Securities).

Settlement

On buying shares from a stockbroker, amazingly enough, you are expected to pay for them. And when you sell shares, you might be lucky and get some money back! Settlement is the dreary, but necessary administration and paperwork that smoothly ensures you cough up for shares bought, or receive a nice big cheque for shares sold (see Account, Contract Note, CREST, Nominee Account).

Share Buy-Back

This is very popular with people who own shares. It's when a company that is awash with cash, having no means of spending it on decent investments, magnanimously returns the money back to its shareholders. How does it do it? You've probably guessed already. They buy back shares in the stock market, ie, effectively from you! The value of the remaining shares in the public domain should then go up in price.

Share Capital

The actual money raised by a company, which in return dishes out shares to the people who have parted with this cash. In dreary accounting jargon, share capital is the total nominal value of the shares that have been issued. Say Bloggins plc has issued 100 shares with a nominal value of £1 each; the share capital will show up in the accounts as £100. Couldn't be easier could it? (see Called-Up Share Capital, Capital and Reserves, Nominal Value).

Share Exchange

Ooh, can I swap my Fly by Night plc shares for your Solid Gold ones? No, you can't! In this context, it means selling shares you already own and being given shares in a unit trust instead. There are some unit trust managers who magnanimously convert your existing shareholdings into units of their funds. Obviously this is only a useful service if it means you can get rid of some 'iffy' shares that you were unwittingly sucked into and swap them for units in a stellar performing fund.

Shareholder

Anyone who owns shares in a company.

Shareholder Perks

My ears prick up at anything that sounds like a perk. Perk? Perk? Sounds good to me. Perks are basically freebies, goodies or discounts that you are entitled to if you become a shareholder in a company. Naturally there is a catch. You'll have to partake of the goodies within the company, eg, spending Boots vouchers in Boots stores. Still, can't complain. They're tax-free and add some spice to your shareholding. The only thing to remember is that it's not a good enough reason to own shares in a grotty company, just because it offers perks.

Shareholders' Funds

Accounting jargon. These are the funds that technically belong to the shareholders of a company, who will no doubt mop their brows in relief. Shareholders' funds always show up as a plus on a company's balance sheet. Don't get intimidated by all the fancy names, like Share Premium Account, Revaluation Reserve and Capital Reserve, etc. They are all just part of shareholders' funds.

Share Options

The owners of these are rubbing their hands with glee (well usually anyway!). Directors of companies are ever increasingly being given the chance to participate in the wealth creation of the companies they work for. The lucky devils are offered shares in the future at today's prices, and they are often on to a winner. The top dogs in these companies obviously get the main chunk of goodies like this on offer, but smaller offerings are not to be sniffed at, as they have a knack of growing over the years into a rather nice little nest-egg (see Employee Share Option Scheme – ESOP, Save As You Earn).

Share Premium Account

When a company issues its shares, each share will have a notional value that is called the nominal value (see Nominal Value) and is often 10p, 50p or £1. Of course, the shares are normally issued for a price far and above the notional value. So to take an example, if Bloggins plc (I do like Bloggins, it sounds such a trustworthy, dependable sort of company!) issues shares with a nominal value of £1, but actually sells them to you and me at £2, that surplus pound is known as the share premium, and is popped into a little drawer called the 'share premium account', which shows up in a company's balance sheet (see Accounts). It's all in the same pot, ie, funds that belong to the shareholder, also unsurprisingly known as shareholders' funds or share capital.

Shares

Usually called common stock in the United States. Other words describing shares are 'equities' and 'securities'. When you buy an ordinary share, you are buying a stake in a business. Whether you own one or a million shares in, say, Sainsbury's, you own part of that company. Owning shares in a company gives you the right to attend its Annual General Meeting, vote, and ask awkward questions if you feel the directors or chairperson are not running the business in the right way. If the company does well, your shares will increase in value over time and you will also benefit from steadily increasing dividends. Unfortunately, the converse is also true. In a worst case scenario, if a company goes belly up, ordinary shareholders are at the bottom of the pile when it comes to being paid out by the receivers (see Liquidation, Receiver).

There are all kinds of shares that span the spectrum of risk. In fact, in the event of a company going bust, there is an order of payout to shareholders depending on the type of shares they hold. It's worked out by priority percentages and is different for each case. The order of payout is as follows:

1. mortgages and debentures secured on specific assets;
2. debentures secured on the general assets of a company;
3. unsecured debentures and loan stock (loan stock equals bonds);
4. preference shares;
5. ordinary shares.

Small test for the reader. What is a blue chip stake?

(A) a new dish by Gordon Ramsay;
(B) making kids eat their food by dyeing their vegetables; or
(C) a holding in a solid British company?

Correct answer (C).

Share Split

This is when a company takes each share and splits them into more than one. So let's use an easy example. Shares in Bloggins plc are each trading at £10 on the stock market. They have a nominal (face) value of £1. A five-for-one split will result in the shares being worth about £2 on the stock market (sometimes they trade a little higher on positive feedback from investors who perceive the shares to be more tradable). And the face value of each share is now a fifth of the original, ie, 20p. This is not the same as a bonus issue (see Bonus Issue).

Shell Company

By now you know that much City-speak is kind of close to what you think it is, but slightly misleading. A shell company hasn't got much to do with shells, the seaside variety anyway. We're talking shell as in not a lot inside. Once thriving publicly quoted companies that have had to sell off all their assets and end up being corporate ghosts, often stay listed on the stock market. Though they are no longer attractive to buy for their growth prospects, some entrepreneurs use them to reverse their successful businesses into the empty shell company. Why do they do this? In order to avoid having to go through the whole aggro of obtaining a listing on the stock market from scratch, and all the legalities and expenses involved. They park their business into the shell company and hey presto, the shell is brought to life as a flourishing concern.

Short

Highly unusually, City wide-boys love to boast about their short positions. Shorting is when the fearless trader puts his neck on the line and sells shares or other assets he doesn't own, in the evangelical belief that their price is going down in the near future and he can buy them back cheaper. Not for the faint-hearted. I would steer really clear of this kind of out-and-out gambling. The way I see it, when the professionals do it on their firm's behalf, if they balls it up and lose a few million, they can always make it back on another deal the following day or week (or get the heave-ho!). Unfortunately if YOU sell shares you don't own and the market turns against you, you are well and truly stuffed (see Bear, Bear Squeeze, Day Trader, Derivatives, Long, Market-Maker, Square, Trader).

Shorts

Also known as short-dated gilts, these are UK government bonds that have a maximum lifespan of up to five years (see Gilts, Longs, Mediums).

Short-Term Investment

How long is a piece of string? I mean, short term could be three minutes to a stocky, rugby-playing City trader, and three years to someone else. I buy with a view to the longer term, more like five years. The only way I would suddenly become more short term is if I felt the goal posts had changed and I had made a hideous investment mistake. Short-termism can infect anybody, even the gurus of investment, like George Soros and Warren Buffett.

Single Capacity

A City firm that only has one function, like pure agency stock-broking or market-making. It does not do both (see Dual Capacity).

Slump

As you may have already skilfully surmised, a slump, in economic terms, is not good news. It is a gradual decay of economic activity. Lower spending leads to lower investment, which leads to lower spending. In other words, a vicious downward spiral. Most of us have not seen one of these and we can only hope we never will. The last real slump was the Great Depression in the 1930s.

Smaller Companies

In stock market terms, a smaller company is anything that doesn't belong to the FTSE 100, ie, the top 100 UK companies. Smaller companies have an upside and a downside. On the upside, they offer the chance for tremendous growth and excitement if they do well. On the downside, if things go wrong, the investor who has shares in them can sometimes get pretty unstuck. Why? Because the information flow on this sort of company is not as good as that for the larger, more well-known companies such as BP or Tesco, say. And they are more volatile, because the liquidity (ie, tradability) in them is not so good. Chances are if things go wrong, you will not be the only person with the bright idea of selling the shares. So when a whole bunch of people try to sell shares that are not usually heavily traded, the effect is exaggerated on the downside; in other words, the price goes down sharply! It's the same on the way up of course (see Alternative Investment Market, Beta, Illiquid, Liquid, Ofex, Thin Market, Volatility).

South Sea Bubble

A mass of investors (or should we say speculators) got very excited about the prospects for a South American mining scheme. The herd fell fervently in love with the concept, and pretty soon everyone was frenziedly buying shares in the company behind the mining scheme, bidding them ever higher and higher. All purely on the expectation of what might be the richest mineral deposit in the world, or some such tale. Other companies were created to tap into similar unproven mining schemes and the ever-optimistic herd kept buying shares in these wretched unproven companies, purely on hype and hot air (does this sound familiar?). Then the inevitable happened and the unsuspecting public became a whole lot more suspecting and started to suck their money out of the venture, causing the bubble to burst. Confidence collapsed, and there was a spectacular dénouement with an awful lot of people losing an awful lot of money, many of whom became bankrupt (see Financial Manias).

Spot Rate

Ardent chocolate lovers will ruefully watch this in the mirror. However, in a financial sense, it is just the current (spot) price of something you want to buy immediately. Could be dollars, soya beans or bars of gold. It's mainly used in the currency and commodity markets among the professional traders.

Spread

'Spread 'em wide!' is the popular cry among City traders, and not for the reasons that you might think. Other expressions meaning the same thing are 'bid/offer spread' and 'margin'. It is the differential between the price at which a share (or a similar financial asset) is bought and that at which it is sold. The market-maker who buys shares from stockbrokers on our behalf does so at a bid price, which is lower than the offer price at which he is willing to part with them. This difference is his profit or 'turn' in City-speak. It's usually expressed in terms of a percentage. Say the market-maker is offering Grisly plc shares at £1, and will buy them back at 95p; the five pence difference is a 5 per cent spread (see Bid, Offer). It's rather like getting foreign money when you go on your hols – there's a price at which you can buy the currency and another at which you can sell it.

Shares with a wide spread indicate that they are not very actively traded. This usually applies to smaller companies with valuations lower than £100m. It is a general rule that as the size of the company gets bigger, and the more frequently and heavily its shares are traded, the spread gets narrower. By the time you reach the multi-billion pound blue chips, in which millions of shares change hands daily, they are so actively traded that the spreads between the buy and the sell price are wafer thin. When writing about shares, the financial press quote their mid-market prices (see Illiquid, Liquid/Liquidity, Mid-Market Price, Volatility).

Spread Betting

At last, a word that sounds just like what it is! Spread betting is just that; you can now bet on the movement of any financial instrument in a defined range, such as whether a stock market index, a commodity, like gold, or a share, will go up or down and this can be given any time parameter. If you are lucky and this goes right, you will win loads of cash. If not, you lose the lot! Profits can be huge, but (and there's always a but!) if things go against you, your losses are potentially massive. The advantage of this type of gambling, from a trader's point of view, is that the outlay of money is relatively small, so he doesn't have to buy the underlying instrument to take a punt on its future movement. At the time of writing all profits from spread betting are free from capital gains tax (see Derivatives, Tax – Capital Gains Tax, Trader).

Square

If a City trader tells you they're square, they're not referring to their dull-as-ditchwater personality. They're just telling you that they're neither the proud owner of shares in Bloggins plc (or a similar financial asset), nor have they gone short, ie, sold shares that they don't own. Their 'position' on their trading book is neutral, or level (see Long, Short).

Stag

I can just feel the anti-hunting lobby breathing flames down my neck at the thought that financiers are cruel to animals. However, before they get too righteous, maybe they've done a bit of stagging. Basically, whenever there is a new company brought to the stock market, be it in the form of a new issue or a government privatization, if it looks like a 'hot' one, some people send in more than one application for the same shares, hoping to get a bigger allocation of them than if they'd applied just once. This is known as 'stagging' the new issue, and the perpetrators are known as stags. As soon as they know how many shares they've got, stags sell them, hoping to make a quick buck as trading in the shares begins. It used to be just a slightly naughty thing to do. It's now illegal and ranks up there with insider trading as a thoroughly wicked misdemeanour. The financial authorities tread very hard on the toes of those people whom they discover to have indulged in this – shall we say –'entrepreneurial' activity.

Stagflation

An economic cross between inflation and stagnation. So it's a period of rising prices and economic sluggishness, which is not particularly cheery for anybody (see Inflation).

Stale Bull

The optimist who buys shares and is very excited and, along with a whole bunch of other people, feels very excited and positive about them. But at one point the music stops, the champagne goes flat, and everyone looks at each other and says 'Who's the next muggins who'll buy these shares off us?' (see Bull).

Stepped Preference Shares

These are similar to preference shares in that they pay a predetermined dividend to their owners. What distinguishes the 'stepped preference' variety from straightforward preference shares is that each dividend payment is stepped, rising at regular intervals each year. Other 'prefs' just pay a fixed, unchanged dividend over their lifetime. Like preference shares, they rank before ordinary shareholders in the unfortunate event of a company going belly up (see Preference Shares, Shares).

Stockbroker

(Q) 'What do you call 100 stockbrokers at the bottom of the ocean?' (A) 'A good start!'

You and I cannot just go into the stock market and pick up 100 shares in Vodafone. We have to employ the services of a stockbroker (or broker, which means the same thing). In the City, the broker acts as an agent between buyer and seller. He passes share orders on to professional dealers who then actually transact the business. There are all kinds of stockbrokers. Private client stockbrokers offer their services to individuals like you and me. Institutional stockbrokers do the same for pensions funds, insurance companies and asset management groups that invest money on behalf of, yes you guessed it, individuals like you and me. If all the broker does is buy and sell shares for you with price limits set to your liking, then there is not much that can go wrong. If, however, you want a stockbroker to manage your money on a discretionary basis, then you will need to take special care (see Agency Brokers, Adviser, Association of Private Client Investment Managers and Stockbrokers, Discretionary Dealing, Execution Only).

Stock Exchange

Stocks and shares used to be traded in a physical 'marketplace', an actual floor where the buying and selling of shares was transacted by a bunch of top-hatted gentlemen (there weren't any women, needless to say). Well, that's all gone, and nowadays the 'market' is an electronic one, and transactions are all done over the telephone and via computer links. The London Stock Exchange is now a metaphor for share business transacted in the City of London, rather than in a specific spot.

Stock Index Future

This is a wild bet on the future movement of a stock market index. As it is an out-and-out gamble that carries a potentially unlimited loss if things go wrong, à la Nick Leeson, you, dear reader, are going to steer well clear, aren't you? (see Derivatives – Futures, Index).

Stock Market

Just as in your local market, people buy and sell fruit and veg, in the stock market people buy and sell stakes in companies. It is the general term describing the electronic marketplace where all financial assets that are in the public domain, such as shares or bonds, are sold (see Stock Exchange).

Stocks

Stocks: wooden things into which you lock bad advisers. You then pelt them with rotten eggs and tomatoes in revenge for those ropy investments they sucked you into. Well, we can all dream, can't we?

'Stocks' is one of those confusing words. In the United States, common stock stands for ordinary shares in a company. Although in the past 'stocks' described UK bonds, the word is not often used nowadays by the UK investment community (see Bonds, Shares).

Then there's the accounting jargon. Stocks are things owned by a company that will hopefully get converted to cash. Examples are raw materials, work-in-progress or unsold tins of baked beans sitting in a company's warehouse.

Stop-Loss Order

When you buy shares or other financial instruments, particularly if they do not fall into the solid, safe as houses variety, it might be wise to put a stop-loss order on them. Say you bought Squidgets plc shares at £1 each. But there is a little nagging part of you that is secretly regretting this purchase. What if the shares turn out to be a dog? You can limit your losses, should everything go horribly wrong, by instructing your stockbroker to set a limit on the price of your shares, let's say 85p. If the shares start to fall and the share price hits 85p, they will automatically be sold. So in a worst case scenario, you'll only lose 15 per cent of your money. You can also do this in reverse, ie, instruct your stockbroker to sell your shares if they reach a target price of your choosing, say £3 (see At Limit).

Straddle

We're in options territory again, so if you're fascinated, read on. In financial-speak, this is a rather fancy way of trying to be on the winning side, whatever happens. Like an each way bet on a horse. You simultaneously buy the right, but not the obligation, to both buy or sell an asset (usually shares) at a fixed date in the future. If the shares move up or down very sharply, the money you make on the winning side of the deal will exceed the money you paid for the straddle (See Call Option, Derivatives – Options, Put Option).

Strike Price

See Exercise Price.

Subordinated Loan Stock

Lenders who own this type of debt are taking a pretty high risk with their money. It is near the bottom of the dung heap as far as payouts go in the event of a company going bust. Almost all lenders to the business must get paid out before subordinated loan stockholders get a brass farthing. By now you have probably gathered that it's better for the health of your wealth to steer clear! (see Mezzanine Finance).

Swap

While this can mean the swapping of anything for something else, in a financial context it frequently describes a borrower changing, ie, swapping, his debt from fixed interest rates to variable rates or vice versa (see Fixed Interest, Floating Rate Note).

Syndication

City-speak. The posh way of describing what happens when a group of investment banks get together to sell and distribute a large issue of shares or bonds to their clients (see Investment Bank).

T

Takeover

This is when company A decides to buy up company B. Corporate financiers, lawyers and mergers and acquisitions teams work on these kind of deals (see Corporate Finance, Due Diligence, Investment Bank, Mergers & Acquisitions).

Takeover Panel

A select committee of high-level bankers and industrialists whose executive may be consulted by companies that are thinking of taking over another company. The panel makes sure that anyone involved in a takeover, merger or acquisition behaves in an above-board and correct manner. It also ensures that shareholders are kept in the know about all bids and offers (see City Code).

Tangible Assets

Accounting-speak. Things belonging to a business that you can actually touch and feel and that are worth money. They are used to help the business to make profits and are not usually for sale, though there are exceptions to this. Tangible assets belonging to private individuals include property, an antique picture or table, a classic car, etc (see Intangible Assets).

Tap Stocks

Taps are bonds that the government has in reserve, ready to issue on demand. They are always 'on tap', hovering in the background, acting as a regulator for the supply and demand of gilts, in case there is a mad surge of investor demand for them. Taps are usually actively traded, in contrast to a large part of the gilt market, which is effectively dead, since many gilts are tucked away for the long term by building societies and insurance companies (see Bonds, Gilts).

Tax

Could someone explain why this innocent three-letter word has the capacity to strike terror into the hearts of the most decent, law-abiding citizens? If the mere thought of tax, or filling in a tax return, gives you palpitations and makes you wide-eyed with fright, fear not. For most of us, tax is a fairly simple deduction of some money from our income (or whatever) by the government. There are only a few types that need usually concern individuals: income, capital gains, inheritance tax and stamp duty. The tax rates might change over the years, but the basic principles remain the same. You can find the current rates on HM Revenue & Customs website: www.hmrc.gov.uk.

Capital Gains Tax – CGT

You are allowed to make a few thousand pounds every year tax-free on anything you buy and are lucky enough to make a profit on. The threshold changes yearly. Those fortunate enough to have more than one home pay CGT on the profits of the one that is not their main residence when they sell it. Ways of skilfully avoiding CGT include bed and partnering (see Bed and Partner) and using your ISA allowance (see Individual Savings Account – ISA). Some entrepreneurs who back new businesses take advantage of Venture Capital Trusts (VCT) and Enterprise Investment Schemes (EIS), which are supposed to be CGT-efficient. I'd get expert advice on things like this, as they are most often high-risk (see Enterprise Investment Scheme, Venture Capital Trust).

But, you cry, I bought some British Telecom shares ten years ago and I'm sitting on a massive profit. They're not protected by a tax-free coating, and I really need the cash; if I sell the shares I'm going to be clobbered for CGT. Oh no, what do I do? Well, don't panic. The government has addressed the problem to some extent, in that the longer you've held the shares or whatever, the less tax you pay when you come to sell the assets. It's called tapering. Don't fret too much about the details, because if you really get into a flap about this, you can always ask an accountant or your local tax office to explain all – and yes, the guys at HM Revenue & Customs really are friendly, and the advice is free!

Corporation Tax

This is the tax that is deducted from the trading profits, gains and income of companies and that has to be paid to HM Revenue & Customs. You'll be glad to know that smaller companies pay a lower rate of corporation tax than the big ones.

Deferred Tax

Tax that you owe HM Revenue & Customs, but which need not be paid until a later date. In a company's accounts, it is something that shows up under the 'Notes to the Accounts' section as a 'provision'. If you are a fervent accounts fan, you will also note that deferred tax pops up as a future liability that has to be paid, but is not currently due.

Income Tax

The dreaded inescapable tax that pretty much all of us have to pay. It is tax paid to the government and collected by HM Revenue & Customs on all our income. This includes what we earn as well as any extra unearned income that we are lucky enough to get, such as dividends from shares, interest on savings, or income from letting a property; the list goes on and on. The vast majority of us pay our income tax through the pay packet using the Pay as You Earn (PAYE) scheme and around 10 million self-assessment tax returns are also issued each year.

Many of us get into a terrible flap at the merest thought of tax and don't realize that it's not as awful as it seems. Those who immediately pop the nice little self-assessment form that HM Revenue & Customs so obligingly sends us straight into a drawer will not know the full gamut of types of income, and the fact that, like it or not, we have to pay income tax on them. If you fall into this category, procrastinate no more. Learn the pleasures of discovering the self-assessment form and caress it lovingly; it's not as scary as it looks.

The actual rate of income tax isn't all that bad. In fact, it's pretty favourable compared with what's paid by people in many other countries. The first few thousand of your income is tax-free (HM Revenue & Customs will wince at that notion!) as it's your personal allowance. This varies according to age and circumstances. Then there are three tiers of tax payable, depending on your earnings, with the top rate of tax being 40 per cent for the lucky folks who earn more than a certain amount (currently £32,400 per annum) above their personal allowance. It's simple, isn't it? Can't see what all the fuss is about. If you are still in a tizz over the notion of income tax and freak out even at the thought of paying it, contact your local HM Revenue & Customs office and ask for their help. Amazingly, they are human, just like you and me, and will be only too pleased to guide you through the tricky bits. And no, I am not being paid a penny by them to tell you how lovely they are!

Independent Taxation

This means that married women are taxed independently of their husbands. The obvious corollary to this is that the wife's tax-free allowance is completely independent of that of her husband. The married couple's allowance is now only available to couples where one partner was born before 6 April 1935.

Inheritance Tax

Doom and gloom. This extremely unfair tax – I reckon this is an invidious form of double taxation! – basically lops off a large chunk from any inheritance that might be left to you by deceased family, friends or even total strangers. The threshold at which this kicks in changes every year with the government's budget; the current rate is 40 per cent and the threshold is £275,000. All those of you shackled, I mean, happily married to someone have the cold comfort of knowing that if your spouse drops off the perch, you're not liable to pay inheritance tax on what they leave behind.

Stamp Duty and Stamp Duty Land Tax

You pay this either when you buy shares already traded on the stock market, or when you are buying a property. You'll be grateful to know that you don't pay it when you sell the assets. The rate of SDLT was changed in 2005 so that properties priced under £120,000 do not incur the charge.

Tax Credit

Next time you get a tax voucher from, say GlaxoSmithKline (hopefully with a cheque attached!), take a good look at it. It'll inform you how much the net dividend was, which is the amount on the cheque. The tax credit is the notional amount of tax that you would receive if you were being paid the full amount of a dividend (ie, gross) by a company whose shares you own. HM Revenue & Customs very considerately deducts 10 per cent tax at source. Since 6 April 2004, ISA managers can no longer reclaim the dividend tax credit on behalf of ISA-holders (see Individual Savings Account – ISA).

Tax Relief

The government gives tax relief, ie, rebates tax on things it wants to encourage us to do. As it doesn't want us sponging off its finances in old age, it offers us heavy incentives to save for this far-flung time via our pensions. A good example of 'maximum tax relief' is our pension contributions (see Pension).

Tax Return

The dreaded self-assessment era means that for millions, the onus is on us to work out our tax bills. Rest assured that you are not the only one who is frozen with fear, like a rabbit in headlights, at the prospect. People far more financially sophisticated than you or me balk at the mere thought of completing one of these. But help is at hand – the boys and girls at HM Revenue & Customs are not the ogres they may seem to be and if you are struggling, just contact your local branch and ask to speak to someone who will be surprisingly nice and human about things, doing his or her level best to explain how you should do it. Fill out the forms I mean! If you're a dab hand with the internet, you can complete a self-assessment form using the free software on the HM Revenue & Customs' website: www.hmrc.gov.uk. There are also commercial computer programs that simplify this frankly odious task. And if all else fails, hire an accountant to do the number crunching for you!

Technical Analysis

Also known as chartism. This is the rather grand description of City analysts looking at pretty little pictures of share price movements in graphic form. The aim is to try to guess what is going to happen next to a company's shares by analysing historical price patterns. Technical analysts are like City analysts. Only instead of visiting companies and crunching numbers, ie, analysing the 'fundamentals' of a company, which is what the fundamental analyst does, the technical analyst swears by his or her patterns and charts. When used in combination with fundamental analysis, charts are a very useful tool for investors because they illustrate price trends and investor behaviour in the shares of a company (see Analyst, Fundamentals/Fundamental Analysis).

Thin Market

A euphemism for 'I can't sell those bloody shares you told me to buy!' I am not an ardent fan of buying shares in which there is a thin market. It means that there is not much demand for them. The thing to remember is that in a rising market, the price of 'thinly traded' shares rockets with frightening speed. Similarly, in a falling market, they plummet, may take forever and a day to sell, and you are likely to get a pretty awful price for them (see Alternative Investment Market – AIM, Beta, Illiquid, Liquid, Ofex, Volatility).

Tied Financial Adviser

Someone you might like to tie to a pair of concrete boots and throw in the river, if they've given you bad advice about your pension! Unlike an independent financial adviser, a tied one is, as the name implies, tied to a particular company that sells its own financial products, such as endowments, life assurance, etc. These people earn commission on this advice, so the onus, I am afraid, is on you to decide whether the adviser's products are suitable for you or not (see Commission, Independent Financial Adviser).

Tombstone

A very large advertisement in a serious newspaper like the *Financial Times* or the *Wall Street Journal*. In it will be a long list of banks and financial conglomerates that proudly proclaim their involvement in a particular financial deal.

Top Down

An approach to investing that involves the fund manager using the political and economic background of a country to guide him or her into certain sectors or shares. Here the risk is that he is not protected in the event that he decides to invest in a company with poor management. This is because top-down investing doesn't involve sussing this info out (see Bottom Up).

Tracker Funds

Also called index tracker funds. A 'tracker' is a collective fund of many small investors' money, which is passively managed by professional fund managers. This means that it is invested to reflect the performance and behaviour of a financial index. An example is the FTSE 100 index. Trackers can, however, match the criteria of any index in the world. A FTSE 100 tracker is obliged to own FTSE 100 shares in equal proportion to the way they appear in the index. The appeal to a lot of investors is that they have the security of knowing that money put into trackers will perform broadly in line with the market, so in theory at least, there'll be no nasty surprises.

Historically trackers have tended to outperform 'actively' managed funds and the costs are low, because the fund is not being 'actively' managed. If the market goes up, investors will be delighted. If it drops, the smile will vanish from the investor's face, because this type of fund cannot use whiz-kid fund managers to nimbly hop out of shares that look as if they're about to fall off a cliff. Hence the disadvantage of these funds is that they are not as flexible as actively managed funds. They suit people who don't really want to pay much attention to the stock market as a whole, but do want some exposure to (preferably) blue chip shares (see Active Management, Blue Chip).

Trader

A few minutes are a very long time in a trader's life. Traders have developed the concept of 'living for the moment' into a high art form. Whereas you or I buy shares with a view to holding on to them for a while, at least months, if not years, a trader buys and sells millions of pounds worth of shares or bonds, or whatever, all day long, with the same nonchalance as if he were trading cabbages and carrots in the local fruit and veg market. But the job isn't as easy as it looks. The real hotshot traders are incredibly wired all the time to what's happening now in the market, as well as what's going on in the big world picture. An obscure event that happens thousands of miles away can have repercussions on a locally traded share (or other financial instrument), and these guys have to respond instantaneously. It's a mind-blowingly stressful existence, with daily pressure to perform, ie, make grillions for the firm. If traders make vast profits for their employers, they're handsomely rewarded. Porsche, mega-bonus, they only have to snap their fingers and they'll get it. If they start to do badly, they're fired. A very precarious existence with no job security (see Arbitrage, Day Trader, Market-Maker, Trading).

Trading

As opposed to investing, this is buying something with a view to shifting it on to someone else, hopefully at a profit, just as fast as you can (see Trader). You will have gathered by now that I am not a keen advocate of trading. I acknowledge that some people have a natural flair for this sort of thing and do it very successfully. I don't, so I stick to plain vanilla methods, investing slowly and carefully for the long term, with a bit of excitement at the edges to alleviate the boredom.

Traditional and Traded Options

See Derivatives – Options.

Treasury Bill

Also called a T-bill, Treasury bond and a T-bond, this is the US equivalent of a UK gilt. T-bills are the most widely held bonds in the world (see Bonds, Gilts).

Trust

A company that is often created offshore (for reasons of tax-efficiency), which entrusts all the assets in it to be looked after by trustees (see Trustees). The point about trusts is that the capital or assets in them are supposed to be safe from marauding pirates who like the idea of looting a few million for themselves. Wealthy individuals or companies set these up so that the assets placed in the trusts can be safeguarded in perpetuity.

A family trust or equally a financial group, such as a unit trust, are legal trusts like this, but investment trusts are not (see Investment Trust, Unit Trust).

Trustees

People who are considered responsible and trustworthy enough to act as executors or guardians of a trust.

Turnover

Other words for the same thing are sales and revenue. They all refer to the total sales invoiced to a company's customers in its financial year. The number excludes VAT and shows up in the balance sheet of the company's annual report and accounts (see Accounts).

U

Undated Bonds

What, a bond with no date on it? Shocking! In the wonderful world of bonds, most of them have a finite lifespan which varies from 1–30 years, and a pre-agreed date, called the maturity date, on which the bond issuer has to pay back the amount of money borrowed to the lender. A handful of bonds just never expire and pay the interest *ad infinitum*. Undated gilts are an example of this (see Bonds, Gilts, Longs, Maturity Date, Mediums, Shorts).

Underperform

When the returns of an investment are lower than the returns offered by the benchmark against which it is being compared (see Outperform).

Underweight

Fund managers distribute the cash in their funds over a wide variety of assets. If the shares held in a fund comprise a lower proportion (known as weighting) than that of the index or benchmark to which the fund is being compared, then it means that the fund is underweight in those shares.

Weighting can refer to shares, sectors and countries. Underweight, neutral and overweight sound more impressive than: 'We don't like the shares/We think the shares are okay, but nothing special/Fill your boots with these, they're going to the moon!' (see Neutral Weighting, Overweight).

Underwriting

Think very carefully before you underwrite something, because it's not as if you can overwrite it, as with a computer, and blot it out as if it never happened. When you agree to underwrite someone's finances or mortgage, to take an example, then you are promising to act as their guarantor, ie, to stand in their shoes and repay the loan, if for some reason they are unable to do so.

In the City, when a firm, usually an investment bank, agrees to underwrite the sale of a large wodge of shares in a company, it basically guarantees to buy from the company any shares that remain unsold after their sale to the public. This could be a privatization or an offer for sale, or it could be a company that already has shares trading on the market, but wants to release some more. Whatever the scenario, underwriting means taking a large amount of risk. Consequently the investment bank receives a big fat fee by way of compensation for the risk taken. If it's a 'hot' issue and investors are scrambling to whisk away the shares, it's just money for old rope, and the bankers are chuckling into their bonus packets. But if it's a dog, oh dear, oh dear, that wipes the smile off their faces. The bank gets lumbered with a huge slug of unwanted and unsaleable shares, called an 'overhang', and the trouble is, everyone in the City knows it, so the traders mark the price of the shares down, which compounds the losses of the bank.

Unit Trust

A unit trust is a fund that contains the amassed money of lots and lots of individuals. This continually fluctuates in size, depending on how many people elect to pour money into it. The fund is managed by a professional, authorized fund management group that employs a team of fund managers who have the job of deciding how to invest the money. It'll be no surprise to you that they charge a fee for doing so. Money invested in a unit trust is exchanged for its units. As more cash flows into the fund, the manager of the fund creates more units and invests the money as he or she thinks fit. The value of the assets in the fund is equal to the value of the units, plus or minus the spread (see Net Asset Value, Spread). Once fees have been deducted, any rise in the fund's value or other returns (in financial-speak – capital growth or income) are handed pro rata to its investors.

Structurally, a unit trust is a legal trust governed by a trust deed. There are both authorized and unauthorized ones. Some unit trusts holding assets other than shares are unauthorized, for example, real estate unit trusts. The latter are not sold to the general public (see Collective Funds, Diversification, Drip Feeding, Investment Management Association – IMA, Investment Trust, Managed Funds, Open-End Investment Company – OEIC).

Unquoted Securities

Shares in a company that is not listed on any stock market. The only way owners can sell these is to persuade someone else to buy them. When a private investor is desperate to put his or her money into a small entrepreneurial company that might be the Microsoft of tomorrow, he or she might do so via the Enterprise Investment Scheme (EIS) or a Venture Capital Trust (VCT). This is pretty risky because there is a high failure rate for young, unproven companies with little or no track record. This type of investment is categorically not suitable for people who cannot afford to lose any money. It offers sexy tax breaks, but tax breaks alone do not make a future profitable business. Experts in the venture capital field are comfortable with the varying degrees of risk involved and anyone who wants to know more about this needs to consult a specialist with substantial experience in the field and a good track record (see Enterprise Investment Scheme, Tax – Capital Gains Tax, Venture Capital, Venture Capital Trust).

Unsecured Loan Stock

It's easy to get bewildered by all the different phrases that mean the same thing. Unsecured loan stock is just another way of describing a type of corporate bond. 'Unsecured' means that there is nothing secured against the loan as collateral, like a building or a plot of land. If the company were to go belly up, the person who lent it the money would be in a much worse position than someone who owned secured loan stock and could take control of the 'security', selling it to repay the loan. Because unsecured bonds are riskier than gilts and secured loan stock, they pay a better return to buyers to compensate for the extra risk involved (see AAA, Bonds, Corporate Bonds, Secured Loan Stock).

Usury

With the vast array of financial loans on offer, how can you protect yourself from being ripped off with unconscionably huge interest charges for the privilege of borrowing money, in other words, usury? You'll be relieved to know that interest charged over and above 48 per cent per year on loans from all those credit card and HP companies, banks and building societies is deemed to be extortion. Thank goodness for that. I was beginning to think that the 100 per cent APR interest I've been paying Loanshark Enterprises Ltd for borrowing £10,000 was a bit excessive!

In the event that you need to borrow money, shop around, ask lots of questions and compare the answers. If you get fazed with all the percentages, like 13.6 per cent APR, etc, be explicit. Ask: 'If I borrow a million pounds from you (well, we can dream can't we?) how much will I have to pay you in total if I return the money over a one-, two-, three-, or five-year period?'

But beware, read the small print. Do not blithely assume that the institution you are borrowing from is going to be terribly understanding if you slip behind on your repayments. Make sure you understand the commitment involved. If you don't like the sound of it, it's best not to do it!

Utility Shares

These are shares in companies that offer essential services, like electricity, water and gas. This type of company is generally (though not always) fairly defensive and stable. The general opinion of investors is that no matter how awful the outlook for the economy might become, we will still need to use all these services and pay up for them. Utility shares tend to offer quite reasonable returns, in the form of dividend yields (see Defensive Shares, Yield).

V

Value at Par

See Par Value.

Value Shares

These are shares that investors buy because they think they are cheap. Peter Lynch, that ace American investor who made the Magellan Fund famous, came up with a mathematical formula in order to apply some set criteria to the analysis of shares. This has now been immortalized in the investment world as the 'Lynch Ratio'. It compares the price/earnings ratio of a share to the growth rate of its earnings per share. It's a way of measuring whether a share is worth buying on the grounds of it being 'good value'. Or cheap as chips, whatever (see Earnings per Share – EPS, Price/Earnings Ratio – P/E, Growth Shares, Income Shares).

Vendor Placing

In the slick world of corporate finance, where companies change hands like so many pounds of new potatoes, there are situations when a company that owns another company decides to sell it. Say Chocco plc decides to sell Glue-it, one of its many exciting subsidiaries, to Woodfloor plc. Woodfloor hasn't got the money to cough up for Glue-it. Instead, it issues new shares to pay for the deal. Chocco groans at the thought of being paid in Woodfloor's dreary shares. It wants lovely cash in pocket, thank you very much. The new shares in Woodfloor plc are packaged up to look as attractive as possible and sold to institutional investors. The stockbroking firm, by foisting these new Woodfloor shares on to its valued clients, has now cleverly raised the money that Chocco wants for its disposal of glorious Glue-it shares. This process of fundraising is called a 'vendor placing'. The stockbroking firm gets paid a nice plump fee for its invaluable work, Chocco gets cash payment for its disposal of Glue-it, and the institutions have been offered a 'unique unmissable opportunity' to invest in an exciting fast-growing company called Woodfloor and Glue-it Enterprises!

Venture Capital

Also called seed capital, it is not necessarily used for seedy purposes. This is money that investors, many of them specialists in taking 'venture capital' risk, use to back small, new companies that have a good idea and a sound business proposition. Seed capital is the first investment into a business (typically friends, family, business angels) to develop an idea or invention. Venture capital is the money used later on in the early stages of a company's life, to hire more people, invest in factories, etc. At this early stage the company is often loss-making or has few clients. Whoever stumps up venture capital money for a business should be fully aware of the high risk they are taking with their money. Even the best ideas can go wrong, and whilst venture capitalists are fully cognizant of the risks involved, smaller, less experienced investors often aren't. This type of investment is only suitable for people who really can afford to take a loss on the chin and not feel much worse off (see Private Equity).

Venture Capital Trust – VCT

Just like an investment trust, a VCT is actually a company in its own right, with shares that can be bought and sold on the Stock Exchange. The VCT invests the money raised from selling its own shares into fledgling companies (see Fledgling, Venture Capital). They offer good tax advantages: 40 per cent income tax relief, tax-free dividends from the VCT shares, and exemption from capital gains tax (CGT) if you make a profit when you sell the shares in the VCT (see Tax – Capital Gains Tax, Deferred Tax).

Saving tax is a great idea in principle. However, it is not a good enough reason to just nonchalantly throw money into a VCT. This is a highly specialized area of investment that needs detailed knowledge of the managers running the various VCTs on offer, and knowing each one's track record in picking winners. Anyone even contemplating this type of investment needs sound, in-depth advice from a real expert in this field.

Volatility

The amount by which the price of an investment goes up or down, ie, fluctuates in value. The City loves to use the expression 'beta' or if it's feeling really perky, 'beta coefficient!' This tells you how volatile an investment is in comparison to its market. The more extreme the up swings and downs, the more volatile a share or investment is said to be. The price of shares in smaller companies tends to show exaggerated up and down movements because it is not so easy to trade in them (see Beta, Illiquid, Liquid/Liquidity, Thin Market, Volume).

Volume

Quite simply, the amount of shares traded in a particular company on a particular day is described as its volume. All companies with stock market quoted shares have a record of how many of their shares changed hands on any given day. It is recorded daily in the financial press, and is also available on the more specialized financial information systems like Bloomberg and Reuters. It is crucially important for anyone who wants to start getting involved in stock market dealings to have a strong feel for what constitutes a heavily traded share. This is one that is likely to be easy to buy and sell. Small companies' shares trade with low volumes (see Market Capitalization), and this exaggerates share price movements both on the upside and downside (see Beta, Illiquid, Liquid/Liquidity, Thin Market, Volatility).

Voting Shares

If you have ordinary shares in a company, the chances are that they are voting shares (though this is occasionally not the case). It may seem rather obvious, but these shares entitle their owners to vote on all things pertaining to the company at its Annual General Meetings (AGM) or Extraordinary General Meetings (EGM). AGMs take place once a year and it's when all the directors of a company appear in front of their shareholders and tell them how things have been going and what the future holds, blah, blah, blah. Then they ask shareholders to vote, usually on boring stuff like re-election of directors and auditors. EGMs are often more urgent, and are held because of specific and unusual things happening within the company that immediately require shareholders' votes. A takeover bid, or the company needing to raise more cash, are two examples (see 'A' Shares, Annual General Meeting, Extraordinary General Meeting).

Wall Street

The term Wall Street technically describes the location where most of the hot-shot American bankers and stockbrokers have their offices. But it is also used as slang to describe the US share market, which is huge. No, in fact it's huger than huge; it's vast. The American stock market makes up about 55 per cent, by value, of the world's stock markets and is unquestionably the largest in the world. It's valued at about 12 trillion dollars. The Japanese and UK stock markets follow behind, each about a fifth of its size. So it's no wonder that the US market is what obsesses most financiers across the globe.

Warrant

See Derivatives – Warrants.

White Knight

The management of an ailing company that is vulnerable to a hostile takeover will frantically cast around looking for a white knight, a friendly potential partner with whom they can forge an alliance, in order to make themselves a less juicy morsel for the 'bad guys' to get their teeth into. Otherwise they run the danger of being open to attack by asset strippers who could chop up the company and sell various parts of it. In the event of such a dismembering, jobs are inevitably lost. It goes without saying that most of the original management is usually unceremoniously booted out as soon as the raiders take over (see Asset Stripper, Poison Pill).

Window Dressing

Some companies massage their accounts to make them look better than they really are for the year-end results. Frankly, anyone who is not an aficionado of reading accounts would find it jolly difficult to know for sure whether a company had indulged in this practice. Simple things, like a company collecting as many debts owed to it as possible and stretching its own repayments out as far as possible into the future, can significantly enhance its cash flow and current assets.

With-Profits Policy

A 'with-profits ' policy is a type of financial product sold and run by life companies and it's available via several investment vehicles. These include 'endowments', 'investment bonds' and 'pensions'. The principle behind 'with-profits' is that it's sold to investors as 'low risk' because the cash is spread between shares, bonds and property. In theory, each year the insurance company that's running the plan announces a bonus, which is added to your policy and can't be taken back. The company doesn't give all the growth of the investments back to the policy-holder – it holds money back in good years so it has reserves to pay bonuses in not-so-good years.

There's been and continues to be a lot of bad press surrounding 'with-profits' investments as they've been heavily flogged as 'low-risk'. However, because stock market performance in recent years has been poor, and because the life companies have had to reduce their exposure to shares in order to keep their balance sheets strong, these have proved to be anything but! Added to this list of woes, anyone who tries to get out of a 'with-profits' policy is slapped with exorbitant penalties, which may be applied after a period of falling stock market conditions. Finally, hard on the heels of the life companies is the Consumer Association, which strongly advocates that the way in which these bonuses are calculated should be made crystal clear, and is critical of the excessively high charges for 'with-profits' products (see Endowment, Pension).

Writer

Back to the colourful world of options. A 'writer' of a call option gives someone else the right, but not the obligation, to buy shares from him at a pre-set price within a defined period of time in the future. If he writes a put option, the writer is giving someone else the right, but not the obligation to sell him or her shares at a pre-set price, etc. The options writer acts like a bookie in that he is willing to accept bets from others on the future price of shares. Writers invariably have tons of money. Well, they need it, because they are taking pretty big risks that might mean losing everything. An options writer could lose his shirt and underpants if the under-lying share price moves against him. In my books, this type of writing is a complete no-no for individuals (see Derivatives – Options, Naked Option, Principal).

xa

See Ex-All.

xc

See Ex-Capitalization.

xd

See Ex-Dividend.

xr

See Ex-Rights.

Yearling Bonds

These are a special kind of horse. Ah yes, I wondered if your eyes were still wide open after heroically reaching this far outer recess of the book. You are so alert and raring to go with your new financial prowess that you know it has absolutely nothing whatsoever to do with gee-gees. Cast your mind back to local authority bonds. Yes, I know it is desperately boring, but local authorities need to raise cash too, not just you and me. And when they do, they borrow money in two ways, via yearling bonds and local authority bonds (see Bonds, Local Authority Bonds). Unlike local authority bonds, the yearling variety IS tradable on the stock market. Just like shares, they can be bought and sold through a stockbroker.

Yellow Book

The gospel according to the London Stock Exchange. Anybody who has aspirations to get his or her company listed on the main stock market has to fulfil the lengthy requirements of this tome. A million rules and regulations to get the company's shares quoted in the first place and then a whole lot more so it can stay there. It involves a lot of regulatory rigmarole and jumping through hoops, which explains why some entrepreneurs, rather than subject themselves to all the hassle of a full stock market listing, just don't bother at all and keep their company private.

Yellow Strip

A rather exotic little bar in Soho. If only the truth were as exciting.
A yellow strip is a highlighter that flashes up on City monitors and
screens that display 'real-time' share prices. From this, everyone
knows which market-maker is offering and bidding the most competitive prices for a particular share at any given moment in time.
In City-speak, it's called the 'touch' price.

Yield

The amount of money or return you get back on your original
investment. It's often worked out on an annual basis to make it
easy to compare the returns of different investments.

There are all sorts of fancy names and ways of expressing it, but
don't get fazed. The easiest example is the return we get from
building societies. If the building society pays you £6 every year
per £100 you deposit with them, the annual yield is 6 per cent. So
far, so good. But then of course the government lops off tax at
source, so in fact, you don't get the gross yield of 6 per cent. You
only get approximately 80 per cent of that 6 per cent, called the net
yield, and if you are a higher-rate tax payer, you'll get an even
lower return. Your 'real return', therefore, is this net yield (see Real
Return). And then there are other considerations, such as inflation,
etc, which also erode returns.

When we enter the domain of shares, return or yield is measured
by the amount of money the company coughs up to its shareholders in the form of dividends. An easy example is a share trading
on the stock market at £1, which pays an annual dividend of 5p.
In this case, the shares yield 5 per cent.

Then we enter the realm of bonds, which by now you know are
just IOUs issued by governments and companies to raise cash for
their needs. Investors work out the returns on bonds using some
pretty horrific maths calculations. The simplest measurement
of a bond's returns is income yield (see Bonds, Dividend Yield,
Income Yield, High-Yield Shares, Redemption Yield, Running
Yield, Yield Curve).

Yield Curve

This is a graph that plots the income stream, ie, returns, of government bonds against time. The City boys use it to try to suss out which bonds they would be better off buying. A key factor is the outlook for inflation, which is the enemy of bonds. At the long end, ie, 30 years, bonds might offer a 5 per cent yield: this reflects investors' views on the outlook for inflation. At the short end (up to five years) bonds could be yielding 7 per cent, reflecting government or Bank of England policy on the economy. In between the long and the short end of the graph, the curve moves around. This reflects the supply of bonds on the market, or events expected by the market to affect the income offered by bonds, ie, interest rates (see Bonds, Gilts, Yield).

Z

Zero Coupon Bonds

These are bonds that do not pay any interest. So why, you ask, would anyone want to buy such a bond? Ah, say the experts, whilst you don't get any income from the bond (in the form of interest payments) during its lifetime, you do get a nice lump sum when it reaches the end of its life (also known as its maturity date). This lump sum is the difference between the price at which the bond was issued, say £50, and the par (face) value of £100 that you get back when it matures. It's why the return from 'zeros' is taxed as a capital gain, not income, so the holder is only clobbered for capital gains tax (CGT) if he or she exceeds his/her CGT allowance. Some people use these as a tax-efficient way to minimize their income tax bill.

Zero Dividend Preference Shares

Just like preference shares, but with one important difference (see Preference Shares). While a bog-standard preference share pays a fixed dividend to the shareholder, a 'zero pref' doesn't. In principle, this is similar to a zero coupon bond because it offers a predetermined sum of money on a specific date, so the holder knows exactly how much he or she is going to receive in the end (jargonese – capital return at redemption) with no nasty surprises. However, it's not clear cut whether you get that money because this depends on the performance of the fund it's invested in. As with zero coupon bonds, 'zero prefs' fall under the capital gains tax (CGT) banner, so the same tax-efficient tag applies (see Zero

Coupon Bonds). As a result of the 'split capital' investment trust debacle, this type of financial instrument has received a lot of bad press, and as it's such a complicated type of investment, it needs really specialized expert advice.

Zero Growth

In life there are lots of doom and gloom merchants; you know the sort, the ones who're always warning us that the end of the world is nigh. Well, they also take great delight in portentously warning us that there will come a time in the imminent future when there will be no room for further economic growth. Economies, they warn, will just stop growing. This is hard for most of us scurrying about our daily lives to take on board. The difficulty is that if we worry every minute about the ghastly possibilities of the future, it's impossible to enjoy the moment. So we don't. What? We don't worry about zero growth.